MANAGING
BY
DESIGN

Rollin Glaser *and* **Christine Glaser**

Addison-Wesley Publishing Company
Reading, Massachusetts
Menlo Park, California • London • Don Mills, Ontario • Sydney

To Ellie with great affection.
Thanks for helping launch our enterprise.

In loving memory of Fred, Bill, and Oraline.

Library of Congress Cataloging in Publication Data

Glaser, Rollin O.
  Managing by design.

  Bibliography: p.
  1. Management.   I. Glaser, Christine, joint author.
  II. Title.
  HD31.G537   658   80–22455
  ISBN 0–201–02717–8

ISBN 0–201–02717–8
ABCDEFGHIJ–MA–8987654321

Preface

*"... There is an artificial dichotomy in business
between the man of action and the man of thought ...
Successful decision-making requires an understanding
of concepts, of theories, of ideas, as much as it
requires the energy to act."*

—RICHARD S. LESSLER.[1]

The *managing by design* idea grew out of my work experience
serving as a personnel and training officer in six different organizations. These assignments gave me the opportunity to observe, at first
hand, hundreds of managers in action in a variety of situations.
Based on these experiences, I concluded that few managers possessed
anything that remotely resembled a plan (design) for effectively
managing the work of others. There was, of course, an abundance of
management folklore, but little firm data in hand to suggest that one
system for managing might be more effective than another. Most
executives did not have sufficient theoretical background to guide
their organizational behavior.

Perhaps some of the difficulty stems from an inadequate conception of an organization's central purpose. To visualize an enterprise
in its most fundamental terms, it is useful to compare it to a standard
input/output system. Figure P-1 illustrates the flow of inputs such as
capital, people, raw materials, buildings, machinery and data pro-
cessing into the system. Through whatever technology the organization possesses, these inputs are transformed, by employees and their
managers, into specific outputs.[2]

Fig. P-1 The organization as an input-output system.

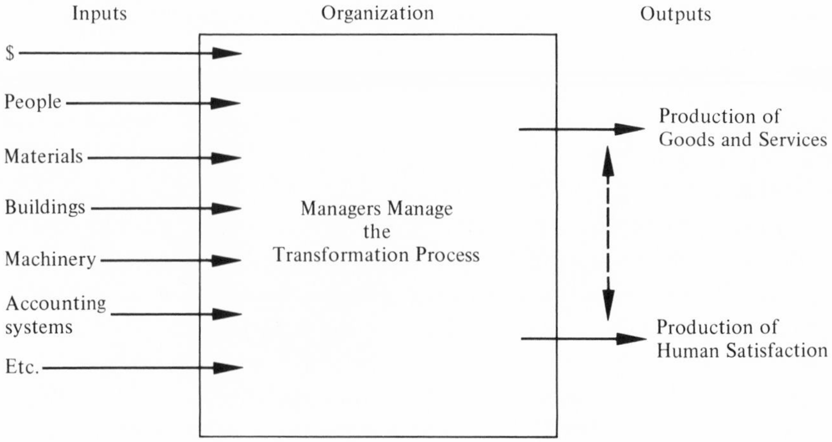

The above model identifies two principal outputs resulting from the transformation process. They are goods and services and human satisfaction, in its broadest sense. Attention is usually focused on goods and services or productivity because they are tangible, observable measures of an organization's effectiveness. Human satisfaction, because of its intangible nature, is much harder to quantify; yet morale, absenteeism, tardiness, grievances and turnover are all indicators of an organization's level of member satisfaction.

These two important outputs, productivity and human satisfaction, must be evaluated when considering the overall effectiveness of any enterprise. Just how effective has the average American organization been?

Turning first to goods and services, productivity growth in the U.S. has been on a declining trend for some time. From 1945 to 1965, output per manhour in the private, nonfarm, business sector rose at an average annual rate of slightly less than 2½ percent. From 1965 to 1973, the increase dropped to 1½ percent. It receded further to less than 1 percent during the years 1973–1979. And then in 1979, output actually lost ground against the preceding year.[3] Whatever we have been doing during the transformation process has apparently not contributed to an increase in the typical American business output.

The problems we are experiencing in the area of human satisfaction, although harder to pin down, are nonetheless well known to everyone who works in business and industry. One researcher reports that "only 13 percent of all working Americans find their work truly meaningful and more important to them than leisure-time pursuits."[4] Most managers can easily chronicle their own frustrations and disappointments with regard to the quality of human satisfaction in their organizations.

Many thoughtful managers today find it hard to judge either major output as acceptable. Some organizations have serious deficiencies in human satisfaction, yet their productivity is satisfactory. Others have productivity problems, but employee dissatisfaction is low. Organizations where neither is very high will probably not survive for long. Organizations where both are high may be judged healthy and more durable. Unfortunately, these organizations represent a small minority.[5]

What most managers and their organizations have failed to realize is the *strength* of the relationship between the production of goods and services and the production of human satisfaction. Unless human satisfaction becomes a primary consideration, the productivity goals of the organization, although they may be met in the short term, will not succeed in the long run.

It is the adequacy of the social system that ultimately supports and determines the efficiency and effectiveness of the bottom line. Until this critical connection is fully appreciated, our productivity gains will be slight or nonexistent, and human dissatisfaction will manifest itself in a myriad of antiorganizational ways.

Assuming that the fundamental unit of change in any organization is the manager, then attention must first be focused on individual attitudes and behaviors. *Managing by Design* is an attempt to answer the question, "What do we know, with reasonable certainty, that if consistently practiced by a manager, can make a significant difference in the results he or she gets from employees?" We have tested the answer to that question on more than 3,000 managers who have participated in the *Managing by Design* learning experience.

Managers working in American organizations during the 80s and 90s will find themselves under increasingly debilitating job pressures. One of the more serious frustrations will arise from the incessant demand (from just about everyone) to *produce more* at *less cost.*

Unfortunately, shortages of materials, rising expenses, and a far more independent labor force will weigh heavily against the possibility of success.

There seems to be little doubt that an American manager who wants to prosper and find satisfaction in the coming decades will have to replace managing by imitation, accident, or trial and error with managing by design.

Gladwyne, Pennsylvania   R.G.
February 1981   C.G.

NOTES

1. Richard S. Lessler, Vice Chairman of the Board, Interpublic Group of Companies, from a speech to the Association of Canadian Advertisers in Toronto, as quoted in *Northeast Training News,* May, 1980, p. 4.

2. Fremont E. Kast and James E. Rosenzweig, *Organization and Management: A Systems Approach.* New York: McGraw-Hill, 1970.

3. FRBSF Weekly Letter, Research Department, Federal Reserve Bank of San Francisco, March 14, 1980.

4. Yankelovitch, Skelly and White, summary of "The Demotivated Society," *Management Review,* January 1980, No. 1, **69,** p. 7, AMACOM, New York, NY.

5. An example of an organization where both productivity and human satisfaction are high is described in a *Harvard Business Review* article titled, "It's Not Lonely Upstairs."

   The article is based on interviews with the president and four employees of Versatec, Incorporated, a high-technology manufacturing company founded in 1969 by four engineers. Versatec was acquired by Xerox in 1975 and today employs more than 900 people. Renn Zaphiropoulos, the president, appears to *manage by design* in the fullest sense. [Renn Zaphiropoulos, "It's Not Lonely Upstairs," *Harvard Business Review,* Nov.-Dec. 1980, **58,** No. 6, pp. 111–132.]

Contents

Managing in the 800th Lifetime

... We are the children of the next transformation.
The Third Wave

ALVIN TOFFLER[1]

When seasoned executives are asked if they feel that managing people is more difficult today than it was five, ten, or fifteen years ago, the response is inevitably a quick and definite *yes*.[2] When asked why they feel this way, most can articulate a number of cogent reasons: loss of employee loyalty, subordinates less willing to accept authority, governmental restrictions on the employment relationship, and many others.

What they are sensing and reporting on is the emergence of the *New Values Employee* in their organizations.[3] In the mid-1970s it became apparent that people's attitudes toward their jobs had undergone drastic change. Furthermore, this change was not an isolated phenomenon experienced only by some industries or in certain parts of the country. It was more widespread than that. Everyone began talking about it. Articles and books appeared everywhere. In addition to being pervasive, the change quickly took on the appearance of being permanent.

Today it is generally agreed that the *New Values Employee,* who apparently is not going to go away, embodies many or all of the following 13 characteristics. He or she

is better educated, more sophisticated,

is more mobile, less loyal,

has less respect for authority and established, time-honored institutions and traditions,

chooses a balanced life, allotting approximately equal time to work, family (personal relationships), leisure,

expects psychic as well as monetary rewards from the job,

assumes an entitlement to a middle-class lifestyle and above,

seeks more open, authentic relationships at work,

insists on personal uniqueness (will not be folded, spindled, or mutilated),

wants meaningful, relevant work,

strongly desires participation in the decision-making process,

understands and will pursue legal rights,

prefers not to defer gratification of personal needs,

is more autonomous, less dependent.

Not every *New Values Employee* will possess all of these characteristics, nor will employees who have them possess them to an equal degree. All workers, however, have been influenced to some extent by the *New Values* atmosphere.

Still, for most managers, the *New Values Employee* is an enigma. Philosophies and techniques of managing learned five, ten, and fifteen years ago do not seem to produce very good results any longer. And no matter what the organization does for the new breed, it never seems enough. The greater the difference between the manager's and the employee's ages, the more difficult it is to develop a productive and mutually satisfying work relationship. Even as little difference as five years can begin to widen the gulf.

VALUE PROGRAMMING

Morris Massey has observed that people tend to behave according to their individual value programming.[4] Value programming refers to the acquisition of semipermanent beliefs concerning moral, social, political, aesthetic, religious, intellectual, professional, economic, and other broad issues. Individuals acquire and begin to organize their own belief system much as a computer is programmed to produce reports, calculations, actions. Basic human programming, according to Massey and others, occurs early in life, around the age of 10 (8–12) years.

The programming, or imprinting, results from the strong emotional reactions a person has to significant people and events that impact his life. Because people are affected by similar emotional events while growing up, the individuals in a particular generational cluster tend to receive similar programming and therefore share similar value systems.

Later in life these values become a filter through which the world is experienced. Other people, events, and the self are continuously monitored and judged according to the standards making up the filter. A child who was ten years old, for example, and growing up during the depression years of the 1930s would probably have experienced the serious economic deprivation of the times. That person's values today would be intensely colored by remembered unsatisfied security needs. Another person programmed during the war years of the early 1940s might have been influenced by the patriotism and the deep commitment of the whole nation to winning a worldwide conflict. In this case, the tendency would be to view today's people and events through the "can do" values acquired during that period. (After all, didn't we create the A-bomb and win the war?)

Massey has carefully chronicled the events of the decades of the twenties through the seventies and their programming effects on generational clusters of Americans. Knowing "where you (they) were when" helps to understand why people with different value programming behave as they do.

MANAGEMENT VALUE PROGRAMMING

Today's managers, who begin to come to grips with the differences in value programming of those who work for them must also consider the personal *management value programming* created by their own early work experiences. Management value programming refers to the gut-level beliefs held by every manager concerning the direction of people at work. These gut-level beliefs, consciously understood or not, cause managers to behave in the organizational environment in characteristic ways whenever they are dealing with a work problem involving people. A manager's values become another kind of filter through which the microcosm of the organization can be viewed.

Management value programming occurs early during a manager's career, probably somewhere between the ages of 18 and 25. There are three principal sources for this programming: (1) a manager's early boss or bosses; (2) the norms of the organization; and (3) current management theory as expressed through books, magazine articles, and seminar/workshop experiences. It should be recognized that the degree of influence of each of these programming sources is probably in declining order of significance.

A manager programmed in the late 1930s to early 1940s, now approximately sixty years of age, would in all likelihood have been managed by a strongly directive and controlling boss. That boss would have expected unquestioning loyalty and obedience from his subordinate. The organization's policies, procedures, structures, and folklore (norms) all supported an autocratic style of management. Furthermore, the literature and management-training experiences of the day, such as they were, would also have reinforced the early programming experiences of the young, apprentice manager.

Without giving it too much thought, the new manager, assuming the reins of power, would make judgments and deal with subordinates based on his or her early management value programming. Other experiences and learnings would occur during his or her career, but the fundamental management behavior patterns would have been established. Unless the manager experienced a significant emotional event during that career (such as extensive personal feedback from a T-group or the influence of a supercharismatic boss with a different management style), these early patterns would continue to prevail today.

Figure 1–1 summarizes the general management value programming a manager might have received during his or her early development. You can locate your own management value preferences by finding your current age and reading across the chart.

When the characteristics of the *New Values Employee* are considered along with the *management value programming* of the manager, the barriers to effective work relationships become readily apparent. Because value changes have occurred so rapidly during this century, managers and workers with a variety of value systems can and do occupy the same organizational space. Educational level, sex roles, geographic location, socioeconomic background, and many other differences further complicate the situation.

ACCELERATING PACE OF CHANGE

The management process continues to grow in complexity because of the accelerating pace of change impacting our culture. Even though we sometimes act as if our organizations are closed systems subject only to their own local customs, they are ultimately affected in both large and small ways by the changes occurring in society.

Alvin Toffler in his book *Future Shock* vividly described the profound physical, psychological, spiritual, social, and organizational changes that had occurred during what he labeled "The 800th Lifetime."[5] The 800th Lifetime is a powerful way of quickly putting the

Figure 1-1 Management Value Programming.

Present Age	Management Value Programmed[a]	Dominant Management Models	Acquired Management Style[b]	Behavioral Description[c]
61–70 years	1930–39	Autocratic	9,1	Strong emphasis on task performance. Firm, persuasive direction. Boss-centered planning, directing, controlling.
51–60 years	1940–49	Laissez-faire	1,9	Concern for people's need for job satisfaction. Emphasis on pleasant working conditions and relationships. Production will take care of itself if employees' needs are accounted for.
41–50 years	1950–59	Compromiser/Conformist	5,5	Middle of the road management. Firm but fair. Emphasize the work *and* people's needs sufficiently to get acceptable performance. The "Organization Man" whose goal was to be "well adjusted."
31–40 years	1960–69	Democratic	9,9	Deliberate integration of people and their needs into the work to be accomplished. Participative, team effort. Full utilization of human resources. "Can do" spirit. One best way to get results. Sometimes perceived as unworkable and inappropriate.
21–30 years	1970–79	Contingent	Situational	Manager's behavior depends on a host of variables in the work setting. Behavior is contingent on whatever it takes to get results. Sometimes perceived as confused.
20 and younger	Decade of the 1980s	Synthesis	Dynamic	Combines both democratic and contingency model to solve long- and short-term objectives. Managers have a 9,9 vision of their jobs but solve day-to-day leadership problems through a carefully rationalized, situational approach.

[a] Approximate period.

[b] The first four classifications are based on Robert Blake and Jane Mouton's "Managerial Grid." See Chapter 2 for more detailed description.

[c] The 9,9 management style was not well developed during the sixties. Contingency models in the seventies often boiled down to random "seat-of-the-pants" approaches. The Dynamic Model is yet to be developed as the eighties unfold.

50,000+ years of human history into meaningful perspective. It is obtained by dividing 50,000 years by lifetimes averaging 62 years each. The result is approximately 800 lifetimes.

When it is recognized that the first 650 of these 800 human lifetimes were spent in caves; that the printed word has been available to the population at large only for the last six lifetimes; that the electric motor has been in use only during the last two; and that most of the material goods we presently possess and use were produced during our own lifetime, it becomes crystal clear that this lifetime, the 800th Lifetime, is unlike any that preceded it.

Furthermore, each major technological innovation appears to spur new and more complex technological achievement. The process is both unending and accelerating. There is no turning back. Figure 1–2 illustrates this cycle.

Figure 1-2 The Accelerating Change Cycle

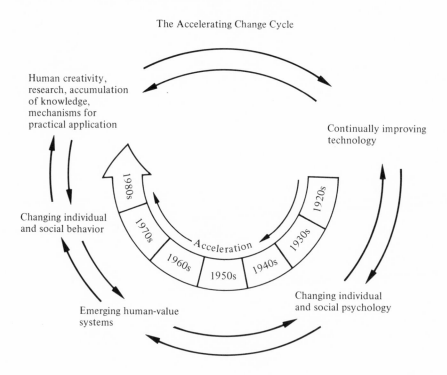

Living and working in the 800th Lifetime is a unique experience, one for which we have had little preparation. The 799th lifetime has left us with few useful models for guiding our relationships. Managers have little choice except to begin the process of acquiring new concepts and skills more congruent with the needs of the New Values Employee that will, at the same time, assist the organization in accomplishing its goals.

NOTES
(Chapter 1)

1. Alvin Toffler. *The Third Wave* (William Morrow & Company: New York, 1980).

2. This question has been asked of more than 3000 managers. The response is nearly unanimous; It is tougher to manage today than it used to be!

3. The "New Values Worker" has been aptly described in interviews and articles by Florence Skelly of Yankelovitch, Skelly, and White, New York.

4. Morris Massey. *The People Puzzle* (Reston Publishing: Reston, Virginia, 1979).

5. Alvin Toffler. *Future Shock* (Random House: New York, 1970), p. 14.

Belief and Behavior

. . . Under proper conditions, unimagined resources of creative human energy could become available within the organizational setting.

DOUGLAS McGREGOR [1]

Portnoy is group manager for the housewares departments of McClurkens, a national discount store chain, located in a regional shopping complex just outside of Wheeling, West Virginia.[2]

A two-year college graduate, Portnoy has held this position for the past year. A few minutes ago the store operations manager stopped by to tell him that his spring shortage had increased over the previous fall. The operations manager was upset because other departments also fared poorly and the entire store was going to be under considerable pressure from the home office. Portnoy was somewhat surprised by his shortage results. The fall figure had been acceptable, and things seemed to have gone well with the inventory.

During a fifteen-minute session, the operations manager implied that Portnoy's future was in jeopardy and his shortage percentage had better be in line at the summer interim inventory. Portnoy is worried because he recently received an invitation from the Director of Executive Development to join the fall executive training squad at the home office. Portnoy has aspired to a buyer's job for the last two years, and he doesn't want to "blow it" now.

Nine employees, full and part-time, report to Portnoy. In the past, they appeared to be a reliable bunch. Their backgrounds are varied, a few are attending college part-time. Most, however, are older, longer-service workers with modest aspiration levels.

For the past hour, as he tried to complete some routine paperwork, Portnoy's mind has been rambling over a long list of alternatives that might ease his shortage situation. What action Portnoy eventually decides to take will depend, to a great extent, on his personal beliefs concerning human resource management.

Every manager has a set of beliefs, a philosophy, about how people should be treated in the work environment. He or she may not have given it much thought or systematically articulated it to others.

Nonetheless it is there and does exert a compelling influence on a manager's behavior toward associates.

A manager's philosophy embodies, among other things, attitudes, values, feelings, experiences, education, training, and reactions to the current organization environment. As such, philosophy becomes a kind of filter through which people at work are viewed. The actions a manager takes with employees are largely controlled by his or her philosophy.

Because of the relationship of management philosophy and management behavior, it is vital that those who supervise the work of others have a clear understanding of the attitudes that govern their own behavior.

Many managers, when asked to consider their beliefs about people at work, report that they have a democratic, optimistic, humanistic philosophy. They assume others also think of them in this light and are often surprised when they find that their own views are not necessarily shared by their associates.[3]

THEORY X AND THEORY Y FILTERS

In 1960, Douglas McGregor, an industrial psychologist, gave us a convenient way of looking at the assumptions managers make about people and their potential for organizations.[4] Theory X and Theory Y are familiar concepts to many managers. They represent two opposing sets of perceptions regarding people and what they can be expected to do at work (Fig. 2–1).

Theory X managers, that is, those who see people through a Theory X filter, will characteristically behave in ways designed to satisfy their perceptions. Because people are viewed as naturally lazy and irresponsible, these managers will focus attention on personally planning, organizing, and controlling the work to be done. Their overriding fear is that if they do not take charge, little of value will be accomplished. Employee behavior must be carefully and closely monitored. Employees cannot be trusted to assume responsibility for solving problems or making decisions on their own. The managers, therefore, must carry the full burden alone. They do it all, or as much of it as they can physically handle within the time available.

As soon as employees sense that this is the boss's philosophy, many of them begin to conform more and more to these expectations. They become unwilling to think and act by themselves on behalf of

Figure 2-1   Douglas McGregor's Theory X and Theory Y.

Theory X Managers assume that people by nature . . .	*Theory Y Managers assume that people by nature . . .*
Do not like to exert themselves and try to work as little as possible.	Will expend a great deal of energy if they are committed to a project.
Avoid responsibility.	Assume responsibility within their commitments.
Are not interested in accomplishment on the job.	Have a strong desire to achieve at work as well as in their personal lives.
Are incapable of managing their own behavior and prefer firm direction from other authority figures.	Are capable of becoming self-managing. Prefer making decisions and solving problems associated with their own work.
Are indifferent to organizational problems and needs.	
Cannot be depended on or trusted.	Are sensitive to organizational needs and want their organization to succeed.
Need to be closely supervised and controlled.	
Are motivated at work by money, benefits, and pleasant working conditions.	If depended on, will generally prove trustworthy.
Do not change over time.	Need general support and guidance.
	Are motivated by interesting, challenging assignments.
	Can grow and develop.

the organization. Little growth and development, on the job, will occur. The manager's low level of expectations become a self-fulfilling prophecy. Employees become programmed to behave in accordance with the boss's image of their capacities. Conversely, a high level of expectation will increase the probability that a higher level of performance will occur.

Theory Y managers view their employees quite differently. They tend to be much more optimistic about what people will do with their capacities on the job, given the appropriate circumstances. Their behavior toward subordinates is geared to getting them involved, creating opportunities where they can use their problem-solving and decision-making abilities. People want to accomplish worthwhile objectives at work. The trick is to gain their commitment and to help them become self-managing adults.

As Portnoy considers his options, the following ideas occur to him. He could:

A. Insist that the training representative retrain all of the sales and stock people in the proper register and sales check procedures.

B. Call a meeting and explain the shortage problem firmly, making the point that "heads will roll" if the next inventory isn't substantially better.

C. Ask the security department for closer surveillance of employees.

D. Call a meeting and ask everyone for his or her ideas and suggestions.

E. Speak with a select few of the "higher-type" sales and stock people.

F. Put up a variety of shortage-improvement reminder signs in the stockrooms and office areas.

G. With his people, develop a specific action plan aimed at reducing the shortage in the department.

H. Remove or physically secure all of the big-ticket items in his area. Keep the keys on his person at all times.

I. Without further discussion, tighten all of the paperwork controls in his department.

J. Ask security to polygraph all of his employees immediately. (Assume the polygraph is legal.)

K. Insist that all employees bring their personal purchases to him for checking and sealing, although the store doesn't have such a policy.

L. Ask the store manager to establish an incentive program for the employees to reduce shortage percentages.

M. Find a way to fire one of the employees he is suspicious of, although he has no particular proof.

N. Ask each employee to give serious thought to the possible causes of shortage in the department and give those thoughts to him in writing. Then he will review the best ideas with the whole group.

O. Ask the store manager to give his employees an emotional "fire and brimstone" speech about shortage, profits, and job security.

P. After his initial meetings with his people, continue to meet weekly to share information and check progress.

Q. Make unscheduled visits to his department when people are likely to think he's gone for the day.

R. After sufficient input from his subordinates, establish a shortage objective and review it with the store manager.

S. Ask the personnel manager to raise the standards and get him better-qualified, younger employees.

T. Personally develop a comprehensive check list of possible causes of shortage in the department and review it in detail with the members of his department to get their input.

U. Closely monitor each person's work and let it be known that everyone is under suspicion.

How strongly Portnoy feels about each of the options, and their priority in a plan of action, depends on his perceptions of what people will do to help him solve the shortage problem he faces. A Theory-X-oriented Portnoy might rush to items A, B, C, E, F, H, I, J, K, L, M, O, Q, S, U. A Theory-Y-oriented Portnoy might be more interested in D, G, N, P, R, and T.

The relative emphasis Portnoy attaches to these options will bring forth specific responses from his employees. Emphasis on Theory-X-based actions will probably generate resentment and apathy toward taking positive action, and may even intensify the existing problem. Emphasis on Theory-Y-based actions will have a better chance of eliciting a positive response from Portnoy's people. The causes of merchandise shortage, in any given situation, are usually many and varied. The greater the range of human resources that can be utilized in solving the problem, the more likely it is that an effective solution will be adopted.

It may be argued that Theory-Y-based measures take more time than managers can realistically afford. When *total* time (planning, organizing, implementing, evaluating) is considered, however, Theory Y approaches often take less time. Getting employees involved in the problem-solving process takes time on the front end, but the implementation phase is considerably shortened because the opportunity for employees to participate initially builds their commitment and increases their feelings of responsibility for getting solutions put into effect. The Japanese have learned this lesson well. Their initial discussions of any problem, because of the extensive participation allowed by everyone who will have to carry out the final plans, takes what seems to Americans like an inordinate amount of time. On the other hand, the implementation of agreed-upon projects occurs with surprising rapidity and ease.

Theory X and Theory Y represent extreme positions. They suggest benchmarks against which we can judge the assumptions we use to manage others. Few managers today are thoroughgoing X or Y in their attitudes toward human resource management. And even though "hard" X was once a commonly accepted view, the world has changed sufficiently so that most managers recognize the consequences of rigid Theory-X-based behavior.

Instead of a strong movement toward Y attitudes, however, what seems to currently exist among managers is a philosophy that incorporates some Theory X and some Theory Y assumptions about people—"Involve people in problem solving, but be prepared with your own solutions in case they fail." This suggests that managers may be confused or on the fence about the "true" nature of employees and what they will and will not do on the job. They are aware of the importance of people to the organization because they have heard that kind of statement often enough. But their own experience has taught them that people can also create problems that contribute to the performance deficiencies of the boss. This ambivalence is further reinforced if top management publicly makes statements such as "This is a people business" or "People are our most important asset," while at the same time establishing policies and structures that imply "People can't be trusted" or "If you want anything done right, do it yourself." The messages managers get are mixed. It is easy to understand, then, why many contemporary managers have adopted a middle-of-the-road stance.

The behavior resulting from mixed assumptions is confusing and unpredictable for others. The paradox is a working population that is better educated, more sophisticated, more desirous of involvement in work related issues, but that is treated in ways that are often at variance with these needs. A stronger, more uniform Theory Y outlook on the part of managers would be more consistent with the requirements of the workforce of the eighties, from the standpoint of both the organization's productivity needs and the satisfaction of those employed by it.

MANAGEMENT BEHAVIOR PATTERNS

To know that managerial philosophy influences organizational behavior is only moderately helpful. Precisely what kinds of behavior are we talking about? How can managers come to grips' with their own behavior and the effects of that behavior on others? Behavior on the job is ordinarily an unexamined panorama of seemingly unrelated events. How can it be described in ways that might help managers gain some insight into their own patterns?

Research from a number of sources, among them the Bureau of Business Research at Ohio State University, isolated two universal dimensions of management behavior—activity directed toward task accomplishment and activity directed toward relationships with people.[5] These two dimensions appeared to be related, and depending on their proportional use, produced differing results with employees.

Two principal ways of looking at the research have emerged. One school of thought has concluded that the research points to one universally effective pattern or style of management. The other has concluded that no single pattern can produce optimum results in every case. According to this school, the most effective behavioral style depends on a number of variables that are inherent in the situation. The effective manager, therefore, is one who can adapt his or her style to the needs of the individual and the specific situation. This, in turn, will produce the best results for both the individual and the organization.

Both ways of looking at management behavior can be useful to contemporary managers, provided they can deal with the ambiguity of not having a clearcut answer to what works best under *all* circumstances.

THE MANAGERIAL GRID

Several systems advocating a single, best way of managing exist.[6] One of the best known is the Managerial Grid®, developed in the early 1960s by Robert Blake and Jane Mouton.[7] Using the two behavioral dimensions of task activity and people-relationships activity, Blake and Mouton have created a grid to represent the interrelationships of these two sets of managerial behaviors. Two continua, each divided into nine points, ranging from a low of 1 to a high of 9, depict a manager's concern for production and for people (Fig. 2–2).

The Grid characterizes 81 possible mixtures of managerial behavior. The numbers from the four corners and the center of the

Fig. 2-2   The Managerial Grid.® (From *The New Managerial Grid,* by Robert R. Blake and Jane Srygley Mouton. Houston: Gulf Publishing Company, Copyright© 1978, page 11. Reproduced by permission.)

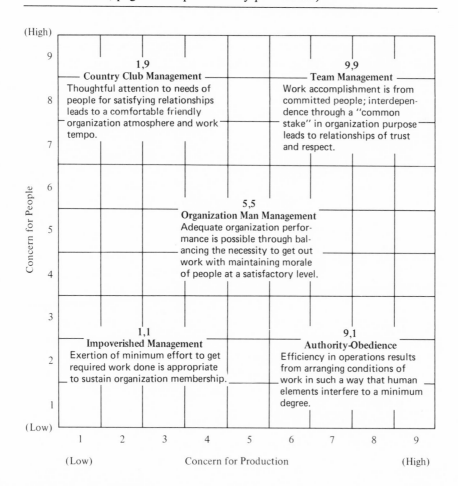

Grid label the five pure styles most useful for analysis by the individual manager. The degree of concern for production (task) is expressed by the first of the two numbers in each style label and the degree of concern for people is indicated by the second number, as explained in the following examples.

Style	*Managerial Behavior*
9,1	Strong emphasis on the task to be accomplished (indicated by the 9) and low concern for people and their needs (indicated by the 1). Efficiency of production is the manager's goal.
1,9	Do not push too hard for task accomplishment, but show a high concern for people. Create a friendly, pleasant work environment. High morale is the manager's goal.
1,1	Low emphasis on both production and the people's needs. Stay away from people. Don't get involved with task problems. Do the minimum to survive within the system.
5,5	Some emphasis on both production and people's needs. Middle-of-the-road position. Stay in step. Avoid extremes. Balance organization's and people's needs.
9,9	High degree of concern for the organization's production requirements and people's needs for challenging, meaningful work. Involve people in the problems of work. Create a climate where excellence is the goal. Democratic processes used.

These general behavior mixtures are evident as managers work each day. The following table summarizes a manager's approach to some of the elements of managing, depending on the relative emphasis he or she places on the task/people relationship (Fig. 2–3).

The Grid gives managers a framework for examining their own behavior and the effects that behavior might have on others.

Figure 2-3 General Characteristics of Management Behavior Patterns.

	Hi T/Lo P (9,1)	Lo T/Hi P (1,9)	Lo T/Lo P (1,1)	Mod T/Mod P (5,5)	Hi T/Hi P (9,9)
Emphasis on task or people-relationship behaviors					
Assumptions about people at work	Hard X	Soft X	X	X/Y	Y
Planning, organizing, directing, controlling, evaluating	Boss does it all	Whatever others want	As little as possible	Some employee involvement	Participative
Communication	1-way down	1-way up	Low level	Moderately interactive	Strong 2-way
Motivation	People work for pay, benefits, decent working conditions	People thrive in a friendly, warm environment	People work to survive	Carrot/stick	Comes from involvement with work
Team work	Prefers 1 to 1	Groups come together to meet social needs	Avoids	Occasional use but not committed	Synergistic use of group
Productivity/job satisfaction	Hi P/Lo S	Lo P/Hi S	Lo P/Lo S	Mod P/Mod S	Hi P/Hi S

Style	Effects on Others
9,1	resistance, resentment, dependence, apathy, turnover
1,9	polite relations, superficial friendliness, boredom, frustration, turnover
1,1	boredom, avoidance behavior, frustration, turnover
5,5	indecision, compromise, unstimulating, identity crises
9,9	stimulation, involvement, commitment, esprit, challenge, accomplishment, excellence

The Grid system also permits managers to analyze their own style and predict with some degree of accuracy its impact on associates. With a better understanding of their own behavior, they can, with determination, bring it under better control. They can choose what their behavior will be. Everyone can make changes if they feel inclined to do so.

Just as managers are often not clear about their beliefs concerning people in the workforce, they also find it difficult to accurately assess their own behavior patterns. Blake and Mouton report an average of 45% error rate when managers attempt to assess their styles before and after a Grid Seminar.[7] Opportunities for comprehensive feedback on a manager's behavior are almost nonexistent in most organizations. (Most performance appraisal interviews are too ritualized and emotionally loaded to fill this need.) This, coupled with a natural tendency to avoid negative messages about their behavior, causes most managers to view themselves through a foggy lens. Managers must be able to secure feedback from others, or from learning instruments, in a nonthreatening way before the process of self-insight and growth can occur.

"ONE BEST WAY" VERSUS "IT ALL DEPENDS"

Many managers who learn about the Grid, Dimensional Management, or some other model of management behavior are later dismayed to find that consistently using a formalized pattern of behavior (9,9 or Q4), regardless of how "right" it is supposed to be, does not work well in all cases. For example, being a participative, confronting, feedback-seeking manager will probably not produce the best short-range results with newer, less experienced employees. When that happens, the conscientious manager feels guilty for not living up to the prescribed model, and the employees feel frustrated because they are not receiving the appropriate managerial behavior, the style of direction they need, to enable them to perform according to the boss's expectations.

Another school of management thinking suggests that the correct behavior for a manager is contingent on such variables as the follower's maturity level as it relates to the task to be performed. This is sometimes referred to as *contingency management*. Under this system, the manager's behavior is contingent on a variety of organizational factors. One of the best known contingency models is the *Situational Leadership Model* developed by Paul Hersey and Kenneth Blanchard.[9]

SITUATIONAL LEADERSHIP

Hersey and Blanchard's Situational Leadership Model suggests that managers will be most effective with their employees if they *adapt* their behavior to their employee's capacities to perform various tasks. This means that a manager's behavior is not appropriate or inappropriate per se but must instead be judged on whether it helps an employee effectively accomplish a given assignment. Because employees have varying capacities to perform the many tasks managers give them, the manager must carefully analyze an employee's maturity level for each task to be done.

Maturity in this case does not refer to age. The concept of maturity is used here to mean the necessary task experience to perform a specific job and the psychological willingness to perform that job without supervision. A fully mature employee is both able and willing to pursue the manager's work objective.

Maturity may be viewed on a continuum, ranging from quite immature to fully mature (Fig. 2–4). Depending on where the employee falls on the maturity scale relative to a specific task, the manager will choose behavior designed to provide the necessary direction and support to help the employee effectively accomplish the task.

Fig. 2-4   The Situational Leadership Model.[10] (Printed with permission of Center for Leadership Studies. *Management of Organizational Behavior:* Utilizing Human Resources. Paul Hersey and Kenneth H. Blanchard. Third edition. Prentice-Hall, Englewood Cliffs, N.J., 1977.)

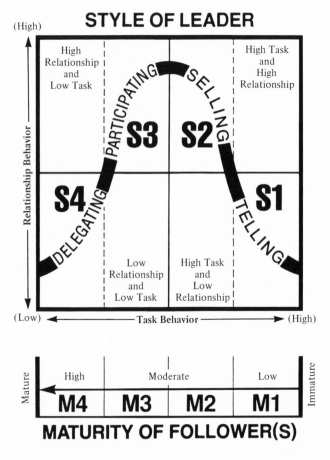

Using a model similar to the Blake–Mouton conception of managerial behavior, the manager will match his own behavior pattern to the needs of the employee. The Hersey–Blanchard model is also pictured as a square to illustrate the relationship of task behavior and personal relationship behavior. Figure 2–4 shows how the manager's behavior is depicted according to the model.

Quadrant

S1	A behavioral mixture that emphasizes how the work will be done. Personal-relationship behavior by the manager, while not nonexistent, is de-emphasized. Quantitatively, most of the manager's energy will be spent on structuring the assignment to be completed.
S2	A blend of both task and relationship behavior. Characterized by a high degree of interaction on both dimensions. Continued information being provided coupled with expanded recognition and reinforcement.
S3	Low emphasis on the task instruction. Most of the manager's energy is directed toward recognition and reinforcement. Manager encourages employee participation in planning and evaluation.
S4	Low emphasis on both task and relationship dimensions. Manager freely delegates, confident that quality work will be completed with little need for follow-up. Manager believes employee to be self-directing, needing only occasional recognition and reinforcement.

In order to apply the Situational Model, the manager makes a careful evaluation of the employee's maturity level as it relates to the specific task to be completed. The manager then chooses the corresponding behavior mix most likely to help the employee successfully perform the task. Figure 2–4 shows how the manager and follower models fit together.

To illustrate the operation of the Situational Model, put yourself into the following case.

Think of yourself as the Divisional Group Manager (DGM) for the softgoods area of Edgebrook, a $12 million, traditional branch store located in a large regional shopping center. You have been assigned to this store for the past year and are well regarded by your boss, the General Manager, as well as the rest of the store management team.

Your management style is generally 9,9 with a 9,1 backup. In other words, you take a strong, participative, team approach to your work, but if results are slower than you expect, you aggressively push to complete task assignments.

This morning, just before store opening, Larry, one of your new, young, group managers, came to you with a list of "people problems" in the departments for which he is responsible. Larry is a conscientious, promotable executive who joined the store's executive training program two years ago. Larry described his problems to you in great detail. Here is a summary of what he said about four of his subordinates.

Lorna *is a new selling associate in the budget department. She is a high school graduate and has never sold before. In fact, this is her first full-time job. She has just finished her initial orientation, seems bright and eager to learn about the business, although the register appears to "throw" her a bit. To date, Larry's approach has been to be friendly and encouraging. He has had little time to review selling systems. "That's the personnel manager's responsibility anyway."*

Clara *is a long-service, merchandise clerical who has worked at the same job at Edgebrook, and earlier in the downtown store, for a total of nearly 15 years. She is currently performing at an unsatisfactory level. Clara is 50 years old and has several grandchildren she is very proud of. She continually brings pictures of them to show her co-workers. In general, her past performance has been satisfactory to her previous supervisors. She has been heard to complain lately that the store doesn't seem to appreciate her work anymore. Furthermore, she has had seven bosses during her career, five of them during the last two years. Larry would like to get rid of her and regards her as "more trouble than she is worth."*

Ed *has been a consistently dependable and productive stock man during his five years at the Edgebrook Store. In the past he appeared to need little supervision or guidance, always giv-*

ing the impression that he would work out any problems on his own. Recently, however, new and comprehensive inventory control systems, developed to deal with serious company-wide shortages, have cast doubt on Ed's ability to handle the job. New forms are not being properly completed. New procedures are not being followed. Larry, anxious to avoid shortages in his area of responsibility, would prefer to replace Ed with a younger, "smarter" person.

Edith, *an experienced saleswoman in better sportswear, performs like a "pro." She is consistently the highest producer in the department. Her kicks come from satisfied customers who return to her again and again for help in selecting merchandise. In addition, she is enthusiastic about the company and helps Larry in achieving his goals with other employees. No question, Edith is a "star." Larry supervises Edith closely so that she will not turn in less than her best, although this seems to make her irritable at times.* [11]

A manager who insisted on following the "one best way" (9,9) would probably not be very effective with the four employees in the above case, each of whom is functioning from a different level of maturity and therefore needs different behavior from Larry. This is not to suggest that Larry's ideal behavior is not, or should not in the long run, be a 9,9 style. It should be—9,9 is the ideal. But in the short term, using only a 9,9 style would not accomplish what Larry wants. He will be most effective as a manager if he provides each employee with the management-behavior mix suited to his or her particular stages of maturity and then makes every effort to help them individually move along the maturity continuum toward fuller participation and greater independence.

Many managers, even after they have been exposed to a one-best-way model, intuitively modify their approaches with their employees. This kind of flexibility may be considered, by some, to be evidence of inconsistent belief and behavior. The Situational Model helps to overcome these criticisms because it provides managers with a rational basis for choosing their behavior and should make it easier to openly discuss these behavioral shifts with their employees.

DYNAMIC MANAGEMENT BEHAVIOR

Applying the Situational Model is not as easy as it might appear. Good results depend on an accurate diagnosis of an employee's maturity level and the manager's capability in playing the required role in the interaction. Constant shifting among styles, perhaps several times a day with each employee, can be taxing. Does the manager become nothing but a collection of behavioral roles, waiting to be appropriately applied to the follower's needs? And where does all of this lead? What kinds of behavior patterns produce the best, long-term results with the employees and for the organization?

Neither model provides definitive answers to these questions. Each, however, seems to offer a partial solution to the question, What is effective management behavior? With some insight into their own behavior, there should be no reason why managers cannot use both models.

The Grid suggests that over the long haul, the 9,9 management style is most effective for the employee, the manager, and the organization. In the meantime, managers are faced with a variety of day-to-day problems, many of which cannot be solved by adhering to a single behavior pattern. Having a rational method for adapting management behavior, such as the Situational Leadership Model, helps to resolve these short-term problems.

The behaviors described by the Grid suggest that while the 9,9 style is the one best way for all concerned, managers who adopt one (or more) of the other styles do so because it is in tune with their own beliefs, needs, and management experiences. In other words, it is suited to the *manager.* The Situational Leadership Model advocates selecting the behavior that is most suited to both the task and the psychological maturity of the *employee* who has to perform the job. That behavior may or may not be the style the manager most prefers to use. While there is plenty of research to indicate that one of the trademarks of successful managers is the use of a 9,9 style, it seems to make sense that managers be able to adapt their styles to the needs of their employees, with the hope of moving them more quickly along the maturity continuum to the point where managers can make more effective use of a 9,9 style. The more managers who do so, the healthier and more satisfying the organization will eventually become. The Grid provides a clear picture of where managers want to go and why. The contingency model helps them get there more easily on a day-to-day basis.

In short, both the one-best-way and the contingency models have their place in the manager's repertoire of self-understanding. The management of people is both a short-term and a long-term activity, one which requires a Dynamic approach to behavior with the manager clearly and rationally choosing what needs to be done. The management process is much like taking a journey around the world. Jet travel may be the fastest method of completing the journey, and we may use it to cover much of the distance, but many forms of transportation will ultimately be required before the trip is completed. Knowing the goals and the general means of reaching them does not preclude a variety of methods being used in the interest of greater organizational effectiveness. A Dynamic model, one that is not only characterized by an open, confronting, interactive structure but is coupled with a continuous search for the most productive and satisfying techniques, will yield the best results with the New Values Employee, as well as with those employees with other value programming.

NOTES

(Chapter 2)

1. Douglas McGregor. *Leadership and Motivation, Essays.* Edited by Warren G. Bennis and Edgar H. Schein, with the collaboration of Carolyn McGregor (MIT Press: Cambridge, Massachusetts, 1966).

2. From *Portnoy's Dilemma,* a learning instrument by Organization Design & Development, Inc., Gladwyne, Pennsylvania, 19035.

3. A manager's first exposure to serious feedback on his behavior, through learning instruments or group feedback, is likely to create some discomfort. His own view of his behavior is often more favorable than the perception others have of him.

4. Douglas McGregor. *The Human Side of Enterprise* (McGraw-Hill: New York, 1960).

5. Roger M. Stogdill and Alvin E. Coons, eds. *Leader Behavior: Its Description and Measurement,* Research Monograph No. 88 (Columbus, Ohio: Bureau of Business Research, Ohio State University, 1957).

6. For another example, see Rensis Likert's "System 4." *The Human Organization* (New York, McGraw-Hill, 1967).

7. Robert Blake and Jane Mouton. *The Managerial Grid* (Gulf Publishing Company: Houston, 1964).

8. Robert Blake and Jane Mouton. *The New Managerial Grid* (Gulf Publishing Company: Houston, 1978), p. 204.

9. Paul Hersey and Kenneth H. Blanchard. *Management of Organizational Behavior: Utilizing Human Resources,* 3d ed. (Prentice-Hall: Englewood Cliffs, New Jersey, 1977).

10. Situational Leadership Model reprinted with permission of Center for Leadership Studies, Escondido, California.

11. From the *Managing by Design* Seminar, Organization Design & Development, Inc., Gladwyne, Pennsylvania.

Person-to-Person Communication

. . . Openness to the world implies a developed and ever-growing state, an experiencing, doing, enjoying, struggling, changing, creating, dreaming, agonizing, renewing, problem-solving, appreciating state of being with self and others.

JOSEPH LUFT[1]

When managers are asked how much time they spend communicating with others to get their jobs done, they typically estimate from 80%–90%.[2] Many suggest that 100% of their time is spent in some aspect of the communication process: reading, writing, listening, talking.

Research supports what the majority of managers sense, that most of their organizational life is devoted to trying to understand and be understood by others. Furthermore, this percentage seems to be on the increase, suggesting the growing importance of the communication process as the greatest single source of influence and control available to the executive.

When the same managers are asked what they have done recently to improve their understanding and skill in communicating, few can mention a program, book, or article that they have read since they were in school. It is somewhat of a paradox, then, that a process that is so critical to the managerial role goes unanalyzed and unimproved year after year.

Part of the difficulty managers have in considering how to improve their skills lies in knowing where to tackle the subject. The word *communication* has been used to describe everything from an employee suggestion box to the way a manager chooses to decorate an office.[3] Communication is one of the most overworked words in the manager's vocabulary. It is reported that more than 2600 definitions have been catalogued.[4]

A further difficulty lies in the common assumption that communication is natural and therefore easy. People communicate out of habit in well-defined and well-rehearsed ways. What is there to learn that is not already known by the time employees become managers?

Perhaps an additional limitation stems from our implicit assumption that transferring information from one head to another, with 100% accuracy, can be easily accomplished. In fact, there are many barriers to sending and receiving even a simple message. I must know clearly, for example, what it is I want to communicate; be in touch with my thoughts, feelings, and experiences on the subject; choose the appropriate words, sentences, body-language setting to convey my meaning; transmit this information through my own sensory apparatus (effective or ineffective as that may be); compete with other noise in the environment. You, too, have a set of noise barriers (internal and external) with which to cope—sensory limitations peculiar to you; you must interpret my choice of words and body language and somehow relate them to your own thoughts, feelings, and experiences. With all of these barriers, it is a wonder people are able to communicate with any degree of accuracy. Effective communication could well be the most complex and difficult skill a manager must acquire.

Because of the scope of the subject, let us narrow it a bit to give it greater utility. Public speaking, memo and report writing, speed reading, and many other communication-related topics are certainly important subjects. But the bottom line is tied securely to the manager's capacity for effective one-on-one communication. What, then, can make a significant difference to a manager's level of interpersonal skill?

THREE KEY ISSUES

Three key issues seem of paramount importance.

Issue one: The act of communicating has a perceptual base. Human perception is much less accurate than we customarily assume. If communication is predicated on somewhat faulty perceptual data, then the communication result will be subject to a similar degree of error.

Issue two: A climate suitable for communication to take place must be created and maintained between the parties. Each person has responsibility for developing and fostering this climate.

Issue three: Each party has an obligation to understand the impact of their own verbal and nonverbal messages on the other person and should attempt to regulate words and actions in the interest of obtaining a positive result. This is not to suggest the endorsement of manipulation or the elimination of spontaneity, but that the parties to a transaction become aware of what they might be doing to each other that may serve to inhibit interpersonal effectiveness.

Perceptual Barriers (Issue One)

Perception may be defined as the process by which people experience their world: how they see, hear, smell, feel. Sensory apparatus, experience, education, family background—these and other factors influ-

Fig. 3-1   Young Woman/Old Woman. (After Leeper, 1959.)

ence our perceptions. Because no two people have identical sensory apparatus, experiences, education, and family background, no two people will have identical perceptions. No two people will communicate about a given situation in exactly the same manner.

Figure 3–1, an ambiguous drawing of a woman, will be perceived as a young woman or an old hag, depending on the viewer. If the previous mind set was focused on an aspect of youth, the viewer is likely to see the face of a young woman. If the mind set was oriented toward an aspect of aging, the viewer might see the face of an old woman. Despite the common wisdom that seeing is believing, people *do* perceive the same images, sometimes, in radically different ways. Because people communicate based on their perceptions of a given situation, differences in perception will bring about differences in point of view.[5]

How does a manager overcome the built-in perceptual obstacles to effective communication? First of all, by being aware that human perception is not perfect. Secondly, by developing the habit of continually checking with others to be sure that their perceptions of the same situation are reasonably close. Thirdly, by remaining sufficiently tentative that positions do not become fixed and unalterable in the light of new evidence.

The Johari Window and Transactional Analysis (Issues two and three)

Two theories, the Johari Window and Transactional Analysis, have gained widespread popularity and are helpful in addressing the second and third critical communication issues.

The Johari Window[6] was developed by Joseph Luft and Harry Ingham as a result of their work in group dynamics in the early 1960s. The Johari Theory is an attempt to explain how people use their interpersonal communication space. When people interact, each brings certain kinds of data to the encounter: feelings, experiences,

Fig. 3-2   Johari Window: Four informational areas.

1. Data known by Self and Others	2. Data known by Others
3. Data known by Self	4. Data Unknown to Self and Others

thoughts, reactions, biases. Each person is aware of some of this data and may or may not choose to share it. In addition, each is unaware of some data, and though it is not part of the conscious effort to communicate, this data can influence the relationship. When two people communicate with each other, an information overlay of known and unknown data is created. The Johari Window, Fig. 3–2, is a diagram of this condition.

Area 1 contains data known by Self and Others. Each person is aware of the thoughts, feelings, reactions of the other. A condition of openness exists between the parties. In Johari Theory, this area is referred to as the Arena to emphasize its open, accessible, interdependent characteristics.

In Area 2, the Blind Spot, the Other person has ideas, feelings, and reactions that have not been shared with the Self. For whatever reason, the Self has not attempted to tap into this reservoir of data. As it exists, it represents a blind area for the Self, an insensitivity to the impact of the Self on the Other party. If the Self could obtain that data, it might provide valuable information for future behavior. Everyone has a blind spot in relationships with others. As long as it remains relatively small, it may not impair the relationship. If it dominates the relationship, it could create a serious impediment to effective relating.

In Area 3, the Self has chosen not to reveal important data about thoughts, feelings, and reactions to the Other person. This is referred to as a Facade. Each of us has a Facade in our relationships with others—data we choose not to share. If we are fairly open, our Facade will not affect the development of a healthy, productive relationship. If, on the other hand, we are reserved, closed, secretive, our Facade may serve to isolate us, leaving others suspicious and uncertain.

Area 4, the Unknown, represents data of which neither party is aware. Many of our unused skills, potentials, and attributes, all of which could have great relevance for the relationship (and the organization), are contained in this area. When two people work at building an effective relationship, the Unknown may be minimized. When they do not, the Unknown remains an untapped resource, perhaps containing our most creative insights and best thinking.

Figure 3–3 shows the four areas (panes) of the Johari Window,

Fig. 3-3 Johari Window.

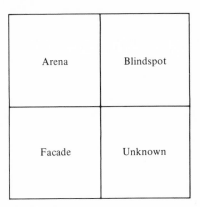

symbolizing the way a person might use his interpersonal space. Two principal interpersonal processes affect the sizes and shapes of the window panes: the quantity and quality of our disclosures to the other person, and the quantity and quality of the feedback we solicit from that person. Disclosure (or exposure) refers to how much meaningful information we reveal. A healthy, genuine relationship requires continued, frequent, pertinent disclosures to the other person. The second interpersonal process, feedback-seeking, refers to the frequency and meaningfulness of the data we seek from others about ourselves, our disclosures, and the relationship in general. Inviting feedback from the other party allows us to understand our personal impact on that person and adjust our behavior, as needed, in more appropriate directions.

These two communication processes, disclosure and feedback-seeking, strongly influence our communication style. Ideally a manager would use both to a great and somewhat equal degree. This would provide a free, open, mutually sharing kind of relationship, one that would have the potential of producing the greatest quantity of work output of the highest quality (Fig. 3-4). Unfortunately, most managers have strong preferences for one process or the other, thereby creating weaknesses in communication effectiveness.

Consider the impact on others of the communication styles of these four executives:

Fig. 3-4   The Ideal Johari Window. This illustration shows how the window would be drawn for a manager who makes optimum use of both the exposure and feedback-seeking processes.

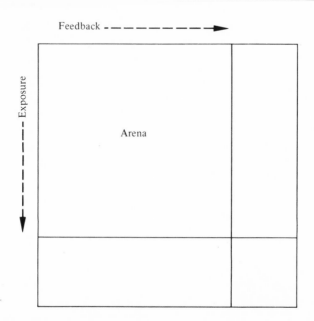

Buyer A: Her style is fast and direct. She uses most of the air time with her associates to describe her ideas, plans, reactions, directions. She rarely takes time to listen to the viewpoints or reactions of others. Most of her communicating is one-way, downward.

Personnel Manager B: His style is to ask questions, to listen to the thoughts and opinions of others. He appears to be interviewing everyone he meets, even if they are not applying for a job. He reveals very little of his own ideas, plans, and reactions. Other people are forced to carry the burden of the relationship. His communication style is also one-way, this time upward.

Chairman of the Board C: His style is hard to describe because of the low profile he keeps. He reveals little and seeks little, preferring to work most of the time by himself. He appears to be biding his time until retirement, choosing to avoid rocking the boat on issues that will not affect him after he leaves.

Controller D: Her style is highly interactive. She explains clearly and fully what she wants and actively seeks feedback from others. She seems to work hard at cultivating an open exchange of ideas and feelings so that the work can progress as rapidly as possible. Her transactions create an atmosphere of strong purpose and high energy.

The windows of these executives might be diagrammed as shown in Fig. 3–5. Buyer A's communication style is characterized by excessive use of the exposure process and underutilization of the feedback-seeking process. This produces a large Blindspot in her relations

Fig. 3–5 Four Example Windows.

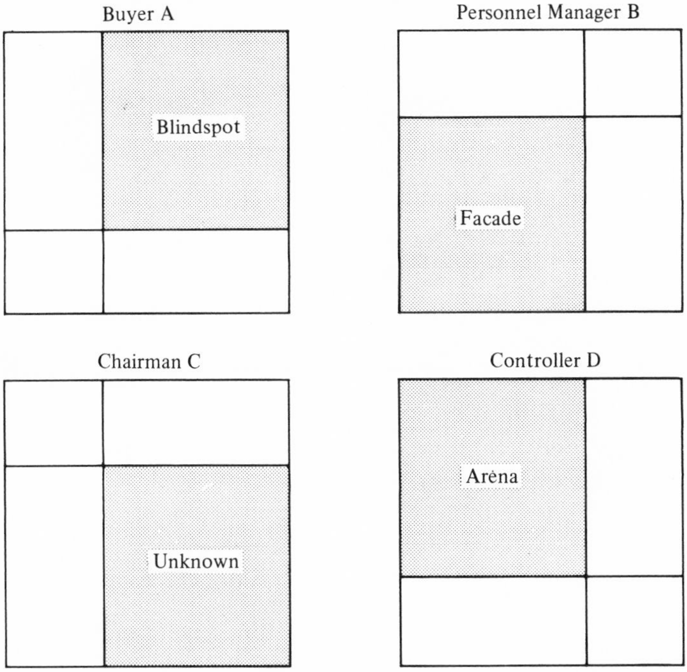

with others. The net effect of this on others is to turn them off by preventing two-way exchanges of information. Eventually, the other party begins to resent not being heard and starts to plan ways of sabotaging Buyer A's plans or flees the situation entirely.

Personnel Manager B's communication style is characterized by overuse of the feedback-seeking process and underuse of the exposure process. This results in a dominant Facade that will reduce the level of trust between the parties. Not knowing where B stands on the issues causes the other party to become more guarded in his revelations. Eventually a meaningless, unproductive relationship settles in.

Chairman C's style is characterized by weak use of both the exposure and the feedback-seeking processes. The dominant area of the window becomes the Unknown. Because C is so reserved in his encounters with others, his potential contributions are not known. The result is that people ignore him, go around him, or vie to replace him.

Controller D's style is characterized by optimal use of both the exposure and feedback-seeking processes. The dominant area of the window becomes the Arena, suggesting a great deal of give and take in her relationships. The effect of greater openness is more solid information on D's objectives, plans, and results, and greater opportunities for participation and utilization of other parties.

By understanding our communication style through the Johari model, we can begin to work toward greater openness with those we interact with on the job. Admittedly, coming to grips with one's personal style can be difficult.[7] Most of us tend to see ourselves as effective communicators. Others, however, may see us differently, depending on how they have experienced us in the past. Only by diligently working at each relationship and examining our exposure and feedback-seeking habits can we begin to improve and optimize the communication climate.

Having determined to seek more genuine, more productive relationships, the mechanics of building such rapport may still cause difficulty. We have learned our habits of speech only too well. Now we seem forever wedded to them. How can we transact in ways designed to promote healthier relationships? How can we get in control of what we seem to express by rote, much less what others express, or don't express, to us? In short, is there any way to influence the process of person-to-person communication with predictable results?

ERIC BERNE AND TRANSACTIONAL ANALYSIS

In the late 1950's, Eric Berne, a California psychiatrist, was experimenting with a concept he referred to as Transactional Analysis, or TA. He found that helping his group-therapy patients understand where they were "coming from" and the effects of their transactions on others in the group facilitated their personal understanding and growth.

At the date of this writing (although Berne is deceased), the International Transactional Analysis Association (ITAA) has more than 10,000 members. The original concepts have been developed into a complex science. Some of the basic ideas from TA—strokes, discounts, games—have joined our everyday language. Millions of people have read *I'm OK, You're OK, Games People Play,* and *Born to Win.* TA has become the common man's Freud.

Two concepts, of the many spawned by TA, are immediately useful in helping a manager communicate more effectively: ego states and transactions—or as Berne saw it, "Transactional Analysis Proper."

Components of Personality

The human personality may be viewed as having three distinct components, or ego states. These ego states may cause a person to respond to the same situation in three quite different ways, depending on which ego state is active at that moment. Berne describes ego states as "coherent systems of thought and feeling manifested by corresponding patterns of behavior."[8] Although other technical names are sometimes used, the three personality components (ego states) are referred to as the Parent, Adult, and Child. (Note that the terms are capitalized to distinguish them from their standard usage.) The personality is diagrammatically represented by three circles.

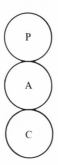

Here is an example of a situation where the manager may react in one of three ways, depending on which ego state has been activated.

A three-page, price-change list has just reached the selling floor. The merchandise is to be advertised for sale tomorrow. The group manager says to his associates:

1. *"Why do they always wait until the last minute? Can't the merchants get their paperwork done sooner?" (Critical Parent ego state)*

2. *"Let me pull together all of the merchandise involved and then figure out how many manhours of work we'll need to finish remarking these goods in time." (Adult)*

3. *(Panicked) "Good grief! How do they expect me to get all of this done before tomorrow morning?" (Child)*

The Parent ego state contains the feelings and behaviors learned, while growing up, from parents or other authority figures. Behavior emanating from this part of the personality tends to be copied behavior, acquired uncritically by observing adults early in one's life. The Adult ego state reflects rational, nonjudgmental, fact-gathering behavior. A person functioning from this part of his personality objectively weighs the facts in his environment and takes action based on the evidence. The Child ego state contains all of the feelings, emotions, thoughts, and gestures experienced as a child. A person functioning from the Child part of his or her personality reacts to the world without much thought, often emotionally, and without parental constraints. Each person carries around an internal little boy or girl throughout life.

It is helpful to further divide the Parent and Child ego states. The Parent may be seen as having both a critical and a nurturing side. A person operating from the Critical Parent may be judgmental, punitive, directive, controlling, or rule-setting. When operating from the Nurturing Parent, a person may be kindly, sympathetic, comforting, or understanding.

The Child may be subdivided into the Natural Child and the Adapted Child. The Natural Child is free, open, responsive, emotional, unrestrained, amoral. If it feels good, the Natural Child does it. The Adapted Child, on the other hand, has learned to do what parents, school, and the rest of society want. The Adapted Child complies, seeks approval, may be overly sensitive to the wishes of others.

The human personality with its subdivided ego states looks like this:

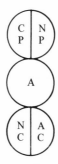

A healthy, functioning person uses all three ego states at appropriate times. An overuse of one ego state suggests a less effective person. In a work situation, a dominant Adult ego state is probably desirable most of the time. Managers with excessively strong Parent ego states tend to create overly dependent relationships with their subordinates. Managers who function primarily from their Child state will not be taken seriously, and a productive relationship with others will be hard to develop.

An additional hallmark of the fully functioning personality is the ability to recognize the ego state being transacted from, decide if it is appropriate to the circumstances, and shift to another ego state if it is not.

Understanding where one's Self and Others are coming from helps make sense of otherwise seemingly random, uncontrollable communication situations. It should be noted that the identification of ego states is dependent on verbal and/or nonverbal behavior. Often the nonverbal behavior alone offers the best clue to the ego state in action.[9]

HOW PEOPLE EXCHANGE INFORMATION

If managers have a rudimentary understanding of the human personality, they can begin to examine their communication patterns. In TA these patterns are called transactions. A transaction is a single stimulus/response unit—a stimulus initiated by one party and a response from another party. When two people get together, six ego states are involved—three from each person. It is the interaction of two sets of ego states that is the basis for human communication.

Three types of transactions can be identified in the TA scheme: complementary, crossed, and ulterior. A *complementary* transaction is achieved when a stimulus initiated by one person receives the expected response from the other person. Below is a simple Adult-to-Adult transaction.

Department Manager 1:   "What time is the Store Manager's meeting today?"

Department Manager 2:   "Two o'clock in the dining room. See you there."

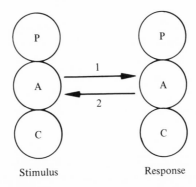

Stimulus   Response

Complementary transactions have the effect of keeping the action going. The two department managers may continue transacting because the lines of communication are open. The directional vectors of stimulus and response are parallel.

Complementary transactions may occur between any pair of ego states. Nine combinations are possible: PP, PA, PC, AP, AA, AC, CP, CA, CC. Below is an example of a complementary transaction between the Child of one Associate and the Parent of another.

Associate 1: "They give us more to do than we can possibly handle in this department."

Associate 2: "Hey, Bill, I'll help you. Just tell me what to do."

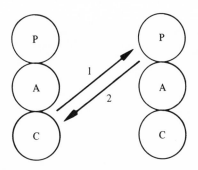

The dependent child asked for help from the nurturing parent and got the support he was looking for.

Crossed transactions occur when the communication stimulus from one person receives an unanticipated response from the other person. The ego state aimed at is *not* activated. Instead, another, unexpected ego state gets into the act, sometimes stopping the transaction cold. Here is an example of a crossed transaction.

Merchandise Manager: "This report just came out and your gross margin is down again. Do you know what's causing this?"

Buyer: "How the hell should I know? I haven't even seen the report yet!"

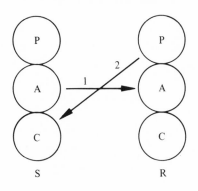

An Adult statement aimed at the Buyer's Adult received a Critical Parent response instead. There are 72 types of crossed transactions that theoretically exist.[10] In most cases, the vectors intersect and the cross is readily apparent. In some cases they do not. Of the 72 possible crossed transactions, four are experienced with relative frequency: AA–CP (Adult to Adult–Child to Parent); AA–PC; CP–AA; and PC–AA. The above is an example of AA–PC.

Not all crossed transactions produce negative results. Below is an example of an appropriate cross.

Buyer: "Why can't you keep these reports in some kind of order?"

Clerical: (cooperatively) "If you show me how you want them, I'll take care of it."

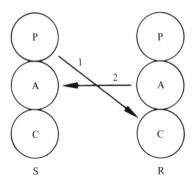

In this instance, the clerical is attempting to place the communication on a more productive plane by giving a rational Adult response to a Critical Parent stimulus. Whether a cross is productive or nonproductive depends on the intention of the responder. Some crossed transactions result in arguments between Parent ego states; some result in the parties not speaking to each other. Some transactions deserve to be crossed to increase the probability of achieving more productive outcomes. Understanding this puts the manager (or anyone) in greater control of the communication process.

Ulterior transactions are the most complex. More than two ego states are involved. In an Ulterior transaction the initiator has a hidden agenda. On the face of it, the transaction appears to be socially acceptable, but beneath the surface, at the psychological level, is a second transaction. In other words, what is overtly stated is not what is covertly meant.

Ulterior transactions are of two varieties, Duplex and Angular. Here is an example of each:

Buyer:	"Let's have a drink after work. I can tell you more about our fall plan in a relaxed atmosphere."
New Assistant Buyer:	"I'd like to get to know more about you and your business."

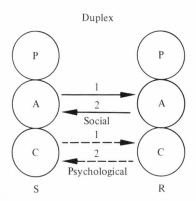

Washing Machine Salesperson:	"This model has everything, but you probably don't require that level of electronic sophistication."
Customer:	"Well . . . I've always wanted the best. You only buy a machine every 15 years or so. I think I should have something with all of the features. I'll take it."

Angular

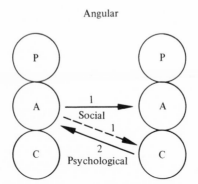

In a duplex transaction two distinct levels of meaning exist; four ego states are involved. In an angular transaction, the initiator is really aiming a hidden and well-calculated message at a different ego state, hoping to "hook" that ego state and manipulate the other person. Three ego states are involved in angular transactions.

Eighteen types of successful angular transactions exist, that is, where the response parallels the dotted-line vector of the initiator. Eighteen more occur when the response is parallel to the unbroken vector of the initiator; in other words, the "hook" was not successful. In the example above, the customer's response might have come from her Adult: "You're right. I don't need all those buttons and dials. Show me a less fancy model."

Berne reports 6480 types of duplex transactions, with only six being of everyday occurrence. A manager's need to understand ulterior transactions is primarily a defensive one. A manager who recognizes an ulterior transaction in progress can choose to avoid being "hooked."

Ulterior transactions are at the heart of all games, although not all ulterior transactions result in games. Berne describes a game as ". . . an ongoing series of complementary ulterior transactions progressing to a well-defined, predictable outcome." The outcome is usually a negative one, leaving the victim frustrated or with bad feelings. The following is an example of the "yes, but" game. On the surface it appears to be Adult-to-Adult, but it is actually a Child-to-Parent transaction.

A merchandise manager and a buyer have been discussing the current markdown situation in the buyer's department. The conversation has moved in the direction of advice giving.

Merchandise Manager: (adopting a wise look) "If the merchandise is not going to interest the customer on the second markdown, you better try to get the vendor to take it back."

Buyer: (feeling inadequate) "But I'm not that important to the vendor. Besides, I've tried that before. Sometimes he won't even take my calls."

MM: "Well, then, have you tried to . . . ?"

Buyer: "Yes, but . . ."

MM: "You know, you could attempt to . . ."

Buyer: "I don't think that will work either."

MM: (silent, feeling somewhat helpless)

In *Games People Play,* Berne describes more than 35 games, many of which are played daily in organizations.[11] The problem with games is that they waste productive time, leaving the players drained of the energy needed for business tasks. "Kick Me," "Now I've Got You, You S.O.B.," "See What You Made Me Do," "Blemish," and "I'm Only Trying To Help You" are a few examples of the many games that use up management time.[12] People who spend much of their time playing games probably need a therapist to help them break the habit. It is not a job for the business manager.

GETTING IN CONTROL OF THE COMMUNICATION PROCESS

Without a system such as that offered by TA, managers have little hope of consistently understanding the communication behavior of others or predicting the impact of their own. Consider the Buyer who faces the following three difficult situations in the course of a typical business day.[13]

Situation 1: Buyer of Junior Dresses vs. Marking and Receiving Manager

Buyer's View: *Susanna, the Buyer for Junior Dresses, has been having problems with Fred, the Marking and Receiving Manager. Because of the nature of her merchandise, it is essential that it be checked, marked, and delivered to the selling floor as soon as it "hits the store." She complained to Fred twice last week about delays in getting her goods, but the situation seems to be getting worse. An ad for a special purchase is breaking tomorrow and Susanna is going to go to Marking and Receiving to be sure that Fred takes immediate action.*

Marking and Receiving Manager's View: *Fred does his best to keep received goods flowing. However, he is servicing twelve locations despite the fact that the facility was built to service only eight. Recent changes in ticketing systems have created some serious snags, resulting in delays in getting merchandise into the departments. The Junior Dress Buyer called twice last week. She strikes Fred as unreasonable and looking for special treatment. He feels that merchants don't understand or care about the problems of marking and receiving.*

Situations like this often produce a confrontation that gets transacted through the Critical Parent of each party. Susanna could use a problem-solving approach with Fred and transact from her Adult. Because Fred is so agitated, he might initially transact from his Critical Parent. If Susanna remains in her Adult state, she may be able to get Fred on the same track, and they might work out an agreeable solution to the problem.

Situation 2: Buyer of Junior Dresses vs. Sales Manager

Buyer's View: *Susanna's department in the downtown store has had very poor sales coverage. She has spoken to Roy, the Sales Manager, repeatedly about this problem and has been assured that the matter would be taken care of, but the situation has* *not changed. Susanna can see that her volume is being directly affected, and now she intends to have a showdown with Roy on this issue.*

Sales Manager's View: *Roy has the staffing responsibility for many departments. He does what he can with the people and budget allowed. The Junior Dress Buyer has been after him to improve the coverage in her area, but there isn't much he can do. After all, he doesn't hire the people or establish the selling expense budget. Being harsh with Susanna won't help anything. Roy tries to smooth over the situation by being pleasant and telling her that he will take care of everything.*

Susanna has been soothed by Roy's Nurturing Parent long enough. It's nice to have someone be pleasant and tell you they will take care of things, but Susanna wants action. Roy's comforting doesn't help her sales volume. Reacting from her Critical Parent will only get her more Nurturing Parent from Roy, unless she makes him sufficiently angry that he begins to respond from his Critical Parent, as well, in which case a noisy argument will probably ensue. Again, the best results will come from a problem-solving approach: How can we work together to come up with a plan for obtaining more sales people, or for getting better coverage from those we have?

Situation 3: Buyer of Junior Dresses vs. Executive Trainee

Buyer's View: *Susanna has had Brad, a new Executive Trainee, assigned to her area. He has worked for two weeks now, during which time Susanna has observed him in a lot of "horse-play." His attitude toward the job is generally not serious, yet he appears to have good potential for the store. The last straw came this morning when she sent Brad and a stockperson to the stockroom to get ready for a one-day promotion. The two of them were playing ring toss with a box of bracelets and a display rack. Although Susanna has made a number of comments when these occasions arose, she now plans to have a serious talk with Brad.*

Executive Trainee's View: Brad has worked very hard during the last five years to complete his MBA. This job started right after school ended, and it seemed like a good opportunity to cut loose and have some fun. The work is routine and not too challenging. To add some interest, he tries to take a lighthearted approach. He knows this annoys Susanna sometimes, but if she gives him a tough assignment he will apply his intelligence and education on the store's behalf. For the moment, he doesn't intend to take this situation too seriously.

Brad's playful Child is engaged most of the time at work. A Critical Parent approach on Susanna's part will only make him rebellious. Brad is not being given assignments that make use of his education and ability, so he feels he has little reason to respond from his Adult. An Adult-to-Adult transaction, exploring Brad's feelings about his job and jointly deciding on some assignments that will offer challenge, will be helpful to both Brad and the store.

By applying the concepts of ego states and transactions, Susanna could work at understanding the potential barriers to accomplishing the things that are important to her and to her job. If she recognizes where others are coming from and designs her transactions with them, she has a chance of obtaining an optimum result.

COMMUNICATION STYLE AS A COMPONENT OF MANAGEMENT BEHAVIOR

How managers communicate with others is related to their overall management-behavior pattern. A manager, for example, whose communication strategy is heavily explanatory and directive, who overwhelms associates with words, and who will not listen or seek feedback from others, probably exhibits strongly autocratic behavior in other areas of the management process as well. This person's main concern is to get the work out, to accomplish the task. Little concern is given to those who are on the receiving end. For this manager, the most efficient way of transmitting information is through one-way, downward means. Managers with different behavior patterns will choose different styles of communication.

MANAGERS HAVE CHOICES

In *What Do You Say After You Say Hello?*, Eric Berne observes: "The destiny of every human being is decided by what goes on inside his skull when he is confronted with what goes on outside his skull. Each person designs his own life."[14] This important truth applies to the communication process. Managers give little thought to designing their communication. Instead they act and respond in habitual ways.

And yet powerful concepts such as the Johari Window and Transactional Analysis offer alternatives. Managers need not be forever locked into their present, sometimes ineffective styles that produce poor results. Change and growth in interpersonal relationships can be made to occur by choosing to use more effective approaches. Following the cognitive learning, skill practice is required. The habits of decades will not be altered in a few brief moments, however profound the insight.

Effective communication in a high-velocity, organizational environment requires that managers make the effort to work toward more open, two-way, game-free exchanges with their associates.

NOTES
(Chapter 3)

1. Joseph Luft. *Of Human Interaction* (Mayfield Publishing Co.: Palo Alto, California, 1969), p. 22.

2. This question has been asked of more than 3000 participants in *Managing by Design* and other related seminars.

3. Photographs of office arrangements that enhance or inhibit communication are contained in the article "The Hidden Messages Managers Send," Michael B. McCaskey, *Harvard Business Review,* Nov.–Dec., 1979, **57,** No. 6.

4. James G. Robbins and Barbara S. Jones. *Effective Communication for Today's Manager* (Chain Store: New York, 1974), p. 3.

5. John P. Frisby. *Seeing* (Oxford University Press: New York, 1980). See also, "The Paradox of the Missing Man," *Games,* **4,** No. 6, Issue 20, Nov.–Dec., 1980, pp. 14–16.

6. A fuller description of the Johari Theory can be found in *Of Human Interaction* by Joseph Luft (Mayfield Pub. Co., Palo Alto, Calif., 1969).

7. Several learning instruments are available to help start the process of self-discovery. Among them are the *Personnel Relations Survey* and the *Management Relations Survey* from Teleometrics International: The Woodlands, Texas.

8. Eric Berne. *What Do You Say After You Say Hello?* (Grove Press: New York, 1972), p. 11.

9. Randall P. Harrison. *Beyond Words* (Prentiss-Hall: Englewood Cliffs, New Jersey, 1974).

10. Berne, *What Do You Say After You Say Hello?,* p. 17.

11. Eric Berne. *Games People Play* (Grove Press: New York, 1954).

12. J. Allyn Bradford and Rueben Guberman. *Transactional Awareness* (Addison-Wesley: Reading, Massachusetts, 1978).

13. From the *Critical Management Skills for Buyers* Seminar, Organization Design & Development, Inc., Gladwyne, Pennsylvania.

14. Berne, *Games People Play,* p. 31.

Creating a Climate for Achievement

How do you install a generator in an employee?

FREDERICK HERZBERG[1]

MOTIVATION

Next to *communication,* there is perhaps no other word that is more often used or less often understood by managers as they define their organizational problems. Ask any group of executives to freely associate with the term. You will get a list that looks something like this.

> stimulation
> excitement
> desire
> drive
> want
> interest
> yearning
> need

Then ask the same group how they might use these synonyms to obtain an increase in motivated behavior from their own subordinates. Answers are slow in coming, but as the discussion continues, two convictions gradually emerge:

1. Motivating another person is more complicated than is ordinarily assumed.

2. There seems to be little a manager can do to directly cause an increase in motivated behavior. (Managers cannot identify a simple "hot button" they can easily press.)

Eventually the group concludes that motivation is something that occurs "inside" their employees, if it occurs at all. The willingness to use one's personal energy to accomplish *any* goal appears to be an internal decision.

That gives us a clue to defining the *subjective* state that exists when a person *is* motivated. Motivation is a desire or need that incites a person to action which is directed toward fulfilling that desire or need. Unfortunately, a satisfactory, *objective,* behavioral definition of motivation does not seem to be available. Does that mean managers are powerless to raise the motivational level of their workers? Not at all. But it is important to understand that motivation is much less direct and more complicated than most managers imagine. Furthermore, it is not a one-shot effort. It requires patience, understanding, and a variety of other managerial skills applied over the duration of the relationship.

If we ask managers how much effort they think their employees put into their jobs, the estimates are surprisingly low. They typically range from 20% to 50% of the employee's available energy supply.

These estimates seem to be supported by survey research. The Gallup Opinion Index reported the results of asking a cross section of Americans a series of questions about work motivation.[2]

"Some persons claim that American workers are not turning out as much work each day as they should. Do you agree or disagree with this?"

The table below shows their responses.

Group	Percent in Agreement
National average response	56%
By Group: Men	57%
Women	47%
Professions and business	60%
Clerical and sales	63%
Manual laborers	45%

Those who agreed that employees *could* do more were asked: "In your own case, could *you* (italics ours) accomplish more each day if you tried?" Fifty percent of this group replied affirmatively. When asked how much more, three in ten said 20% more.

The subject of motivation is clearly an important one. Books, articles, and seminars all devote some attention to the subject.

The practical application for all this theory, however, is dismally sparse. Most managers do not have a plan (design) for improving the motivational climate for their employees.

To illustrate that many managers rely on motivation folklore, we ask managers in our seminars to put themselves in the shoes of their hourly paid associates and rank a list of items in terms of their job-related importance. Five of those items are listed in Fig. 4–1. When rankings are averaged, items one, two and three are usually found at the top of the list. These items represent what many managers believe motivates hourly paid employees.

Figure 4-1   What Do People Want Most from Their Jobs?

1. Good wages/salaries/benefits

2. Job security

3. Good working conditions

4. Opportunity for promotion and growth within the organization

5. Interesting, challenging work.

In 1973 and 1974 the National Opinion Research Center conducted two nationwide surveys of 749 workers, including both white- and blue-collar employees, to find out what people really wanted from their jobs. Figure 4–2 summarizes their findings.[3]

Fig. 4-2   National Opinion Research Center findings: What do people want most from their jobs?

High income	15.75%
No danger of being fired	7.61%
Short work hours and much free time	5.34%
Chances for advancement	18.42%
Important and meaningful work	52.88%

Important and meaningful work was, on the average, of greater concern than the other four characteristics combined. When the rankings from our informal manager surveys are compared to the employee responses in this survey, it is immediately apparent that managers and subordinates have vastly different perceptions concerning what is important to rank-and-file workers.

If managers base their motivational efforts on their faulty perceptions of what motivates their employees, it is easy to see how ineffective their actions might be. The low level of energy being brought to bear on organizational objectives is, at least partially, the result of the managers's lack of clarity concerning those factors that will create a more productive and satisfying work climate.

MASLOW AND HERZBERG

Although many people have theorized on the subject of human motivation, the thinking of two men, Abraham Maslow and Frederick Herzberg, continues to offer managers practical help in this area. Abraham Maslow was a psychologist and writer who contributed greatly to our understanding of human needs and how these needs affect goal-directed behavior. Maslow's writing has been widely published and read.

Frederick Herzberg, also a psychologist and writer, researched and developed the Hygiene-Motivation Theory. Herzberg's work has practical application to the process of job enrichment.

It is not our intention to repeat what has already been adequately treated in other sources, but to attempt to fit both Maslow and Herzberg into the framework of the Managing by Design system.

THE HIERARCHY OF NEEDS

Maslow has observed that every person, at any given point in time, has a number of competing needs. He may feel hungry, insecure, lonely, unappreciated, and desirous of an opportunity to express a creative drive. One of these needs will be stronger than the others and will therefore command his attention. This need sets up a state of tension within the individual that remains until something is done to abate that need. In other words, a person's needs serve as prods to move him toward specific goals that will satisfy those needs.

Managers who understand their employees' needs can encourage them to exert more of their energy in the accomplishment of organizational objectives, in ways that will also satisfy their individual needs. Maslow's Hierarchy of Needs model offers a very practical way of looking at motivational issues in an organization.

A brief review of the Hierarchy of Needs Theory shows that Maslow saw human needs as organizing themselves into five levels.

One might imagine them arranged in the form of a hierarchy because each need requires a degree of satisfaction before the next higher level can receive attention. The hierarchy is often pictured as a triangle[4] (Fig. 4–3).

Fig. 4–3 Maslow's Hierarchy of Needs.

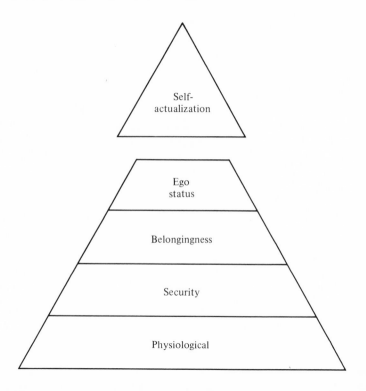

The five need levels may be separated into generalized personal needs and organizational needs. Figure 4–4 suggests some of the possible goal objects for each level.

Various ways of representing the five need systems have been devised. All attempt to convey the stair–step arrangement of the need levels. The lower step must be successfully negotiated before the next higher step can be reached. Figure 4–3 is drawn so that Self-Actualization Needs, shown at the top of the pyramid, are emphasized. People's needs to self-actualize at work and in their private lives are more significant than most managers realize.

Figure 4-4 Personal and Organizational Goal Objects.

Need Level	General Personal Needs	General Organizational Needs
Physiological	Food, clothing, shelter, sex, health	Pay,* pleasant, comfortable working conditions
Security	Freedom from deprivation/harm, predictability, means to continue present life style	Job security, benefits, standardized policies and procedures, ordered environment, union contract
Belongingness	Companionship, love, friendship, club/church/community membership	Harmonious working relationships, informal gatherings, organized sport/recreational activities, picnics
Ego Status	Public recognition for accomplishment, community/club offices	Titles, awards, companywide recognition, perquisites, office decor
Self-Actualization	Creative hobbies, self-expression, opportunities for growth, challenge, independence	Challenging assignments, autonomy in problem-solving and decision-making, opportunity to be creative and experience professional growth

* Pay can conceivably satisfy individual needs at every level. One can imagine a person even self-actualizing over money. Money is a very complex motivator and its position depends wholly on where in the hierarchy an individual chooses to place it.

Several important implications may be drawn from the Maslow model.

1. All people (and this applies to all employees) have *all* of the needs on the pyramid. If managers are asked to rank the items listed in Fig. 4-1 in terms of their own preferences, 4 and 5 are usually at the top of the list. Managers generally see these same items as being less important for hourly paid employees. This suggests that managers assume that hourly paid employees do not have the same needs as managers. Employees do have them, but satisfaction of the higher-level needs, Esteem and Self Actualization, generally takes place *away* from the job. Much of the work offered to rank-and-file employees does not provide opportunities for satisfaction of higher-level needs. It is interesting to speculate how much more productive and satisfied hourly paid employees might be if those opportunities existed at work.

2. People progress up the pyramid when they achieve a relative degree of satisfaction at their current level. This means that employees who are concerned about job security will be relatively unconcerned about having satisfying working relationships with their peers until they feel that they have "steady" work and that a weekly paycheck is assured.

3. People have differing need strengths and will spend more or less time at each level, depending on what it takes to find a relative degree of satisfaction at each level.

4. The pyramid should be regarded as somewhat fluid. It is possible to be operating at the highest level, when suddenly circumstances change and lower-level needs become prepotent again. This probably happens each time an employee gets a new boss. The employee may have been gratifying Self-Actualization needs but now becomes concerned about job security with the arrival of the new boss.

5. Only unsatisfied needs are useful for harnessing an employee's energy and commitment. If retirement worries are not an issue for a specific individual, that person is not likely to be impressed with an improved pension plan or other means of securing his or her future. An employee who feels relatively well-insured will not feel more motivated when the company announces greater

group-insurance coverage. In other words, people do not expend additional energy on already satisfied needs.

6. Managers have only limited control over the objects that satisfy lower-level needs. If a pay range is an irritant to an employee, a single manager in a large organization may not be able to do much about getting it changed. On the other hand, managers do have enormous power over the satisfaction of higher-level needs. Work can be made more interesting. Recognition for accomplishment can be provided. The most influential satisfiers are still in the hands of the manager. Managers of unionized workgroups frequently complain about their inability to motivate people under contract. In terms of the Hierarchy, unions control needs at the first two or three levels only, leaving managers in control of the more potent elements of job satisfaction.

APPLYING THE HIERARCHY

Theories are useful in that they help managers make sense out of their world. Without theories or a framework for looking at the management process, it is very difficult to predict with accuracy the impact of events and people on the organization as a whole.

Consider the following case example.[5] Armed with the Maslow model, Martha could quickly start her diagnosis and plan her course of action.

Case

Martha is the department manager for Lingerie and Sleepwear. She has held this position for the past two years. During this time her volume has slowly but steadily eroded, despite the efforts of the store and the merchandising staff to apply first aid to the weakening sales trends. The Store Manager has told Martha that her job is in jeopardy. Unless she can get her department moving in the right direction, he will have to find someone who can.

Martha is conscientious and anxious to do a professional job. At the moment, she is disappointed in herself and her staff, which she regards as the primary cause for her failures. She seems to command little respect from her employees and has been gradually losing them to other stores. Five of her key people are described below.

Ralph: *Ralph is the genial stock person for the department. He is in his fifties and appears to be relatively satisfied with his station in life. Now, however, he seems to be taking more than his allotted time for breaks and lunches. He cannot be found when he is most needed. Ralph's stockrooms are in a remote corner of the store's fourth basement. Few opportunities for contact with co-workers exist for Ralph during long periods of the day. The death of his wife seemed to coincide with his declining performance, although this occurred well over a year ago.*

Jessie: *Jessie attends a local college full time. She works as a contingent sales associate in lingerie. She has held this position for the past year. Until recently, her performance was above average. Lately she seems less cooperative and flexible. She has complained several times to her co-workers about her hourly pay rate. She has expressed the belief that she is underpaid in comparison to other girls she knows at school who are doing similar work in other stores. She has been thinking of taking another job so that she can meet her college expenses.*

Judy: *Judy is also a part-time regular sales associate. She has been with the store for two and a half years. Previously, she worked for a competitor as an assistant buyer. Her performance, although adequate, could be more productive. She has two years of college and feels that she should be doing more with her life. On several occasions, she has asked for more responsibility. When Martha is not present, Judy tries to give customers the impression that she is the department manager.*

Joan: *Joan, a full-time sales associate, has worked in the department for fifteen years and has just had her sixtieth birthday. She is one of the longest-service employees in the store. Her performance has been satisfactory, but lately she has missed some time because of illness. On a number of occasions, she has expressed concern about her job security to her co-*

workers. She fears that she will be replaced because of her age. She seems very nervous and insecure around customers, behavior that did not characterize her in the past.

Frederica: *Frederica is a full-time sales associate, with eight years of service, who apparently does not "need" to work, but who consistently performs at a high level. Her only fault appears to be her strong desire for more responsibility and challenging assignments. She is very vocal about this to anyone who will listen. She sometimes turns off customers who don't want to get involved.*

The five situations above may be considered from the viewpoint of the Hierarchy of Needs. For example, Martha might quickly come to the conclusion that Ralph, because he is approaching retirement age, just doesn't care as much about his job anymore. Applying some pressure, maybe threatening the loss of his job, would "shape him up a bit." However, if she looks more closely at Ralph's situation, it should become apparent that he is expressing a need for social interaction. He may always have had some dissatisfaction with his isolated work area; but the loss of his wife has compounded his feelings of loneliness until the situation has become intolerable for him. Ralph will not be able to put more effort into regaining his earlier performance level until his needs for human contact, on the job, are dealt with.

It would be too easy to label Jessie as an uncooperative person. It is not likely that her position as a contingent sales associate offers her sufficient nonmonetary rewards to compensate for her pay level, which she knows is not competitive with other stores. Money is the important concern for Jessie at this particular time because she needs a fixed amount to cover her college expenses. She will no doubt seek other employment unless her wages are made equal to what she could earn elsewhere. Once that condition is met, Jessie will probably begin to focus on the next level of the Hierarchy, the need for job security.

Although Judy presently is able to work only part-time, her educational background and previous work experience probably qualify her for increased responsibility in her present job. There is an important additional factor—she feels she should be accomplishing more in her life. Martha could certainly help increase Judy's level of productivity by either restructuring the job or giving Judy additional responsibility, which would utilize more of her capacity.

Joan is not unlike many of the employees found in organizations today. She needs to be reassured that her job is not in jeopardy because of her age or her recent illness. It would be further helpful if Martha reconfirmed Joan's value to the company based on her fifteen years of satisfactory service.

If Martha properly channeled Frederica's drive, she could use that energy and eight years of experience to good advantage. Martha is relatively new to her position, and no doubt Frederica has information, experience, and creative ideas that could be beneficial to Martha and the entire department, if she were allowed to express them. Creating opportunities for Frederica to participate in the plans for the department, adding increased responsibility, perhaps making her the Assistant Department Manager, would help satisfy Frederica's needs for more challenge.

The success a manager experiences in taking action depends on the accuracy of his or her diagnosis. Many times only specific, careful probing *with* the employee will identify the employee's most important need. The crucial role the manager must perform is to specifically connect that need with the goals inherent in the work itself. If the employee is experiencing strong self-esteem needs, then the manager must help that person see how those needs can be satisfied through his or her work.

At the same time, it should be pointed out that occasionally jobs cannot and will not afford the employee an opportunity to satisfy certain needs. An example might be a salary requirement that exceeds what a job can reasonably be expected to pay. The manager has the responsibility for clarifying that as well. Not every strongly felt need, no matter how legitimate, can be satisfied on the job. Many can, however, and that's the manager's task.

DEFICIT NEEDS AND GROWTH NEEDS

As the five need levels are considered, it should become apparent that the expenditure of energy at the higher levels is more satisfying for the employee and more constructive for the organization. Employees with persistent, unsatisfied needs at lower levels have little time or energy to think and work creatively for either themselves or the company. The employee's best efforts are lost as he or she attempts to deal with the issues of pay, benefits, working conditions, or some belongingness needs. The more the employee's attention can be turned to problem-solving, to meeting difficult challenges, to using his or her imagination, the more effective that worker will be in terms of helping the company meet its productivity goals.

Maslow identified the first four levels as *deficit needs*. Deficit needs cause people to focus most of their energy on reaching goals that are not very satisfying in the long run. For example, if my self-esteem is a key issue, then I must work very hard to prove that I am worthy. If I am insecure, then I expend a great deal of energy in trying to stabilize my position in the organization. Satisfying deficit needs keeps me from growing as an individual. I can work at relieving physiological discomfort, but I do not experience health in the fullest sense of the word.

Psychologically healthy people have sufficiently satisfied their deficit needs and are able to expend more energy at the fifth level, being primarily motivated by opportunities to self-actualize. Only those activities that allow us to self-actualize will promote health, growth, and development—in short, make us more fully human.

Self-Actualization is a difficult term to define. Nonetheless, managers need at least a general understanding of the concept if they are to make use of it in the supervision of others. Maslow defined Self-Actualization as the ". . . ongoing actualization of potentials, capacities, talents, as fulfillment of mission (call, fate, destiny, vocation) . . . fuller knowledge of and acceptance of the person's own intrinsic nature, unceasing trend toward unity, integration, or synergy."[6] Maslow considered growth, individuation, autonomy, self-development, productiveness, self-realization, integration, and creativity all roughly synonomous with Self-Actualization.

Maslow defined "healthy people" as having these thirteen observable characteristics.[7]

- Superior perception of reality

- Increased acceptance of self, of others, and of nature

- Increased spontaneity

- Increase in problem centering

- Increased detachment and desire for privacy

- Increased autonomy and resistance to enculturation

- Greater freshness of appreciation, and richness of emotional reaction

- Higher frequency of peak experiences ("moments of highest happiness and fulfillment")

- Increased identification with the human species

- Changed interpersonal relations

- More democratic character structure

- Greatly increased creativeness

- Certain changes in the value system

Managers who are able to arrange the working conditions of their employees so that they can develop these characteristics more fully will have performed a great service for the employees as well as for the organization. A satisfying work environment is one where there are widespread opportunities for employees to self-actualize.

Managers usually have significant opportunities in their own jobs to experience self-actualization gratification. They use their imaginations, face and solve difficult and challenging problems. They plan, organize, evaluate, create, and experience the joys of real achievement. Over a period of time they may look back and take pleasure in their department or organization's accomplishments. If these self-actualization opportunities fall into short supply or become unavailable, they may go elsewhere in search of new "challenges."

Unfortunately, the same opportunities are often not available to hourly paid personnel. Their jobs frequently are empty of creativity, their work is overplanned and overorganized, their autonomy is carefully limited in the names of efficiency and control. Under these circumstances, rank-and-file employees look elsewhere for their kicks. In short, they self-actualize away from the job. Their best energies go into their avocations, after business hours.

This is not to suggest that people should not self-actualize off the job but that valuable human energy is being lost by many organizations. If managers could help their employees move through the lower need levels, that is, achieve relative satisfaction of their deficit needs and provide opportunities for satisfying their growth needs, two important things would happen. First of all, the organization would begin to get the best of what people have to offer. Secondly, people would find their work more exciting, more of a "turn on." In effect, the manager would be simultaneously promoting individual *and* organizational health.

Unlike needs at the four lower levels, growth is a never ending source of organizational vitality. Lower-level needs can reach satiety. How much job security does an employee need before he or she begins a quest for new fulfillments? Growth needs, however, expand as they are fed. They may never be fully satisfied, although a great sense of accomplishment will ensue during the process. More and more energy is voluntarily poured into their achievement.

MOTIVATION–HYGIENE (M–H) THEORY

Maslow's theory is not perfect, that is, it will not answer all of a manager's questions about motivation. But it does provide a helpful starting point. Frederick Herzberg's Motivation–Hygiene Theory provides an additional, and perhaps more practical, perspective.

The beginning of the M–H Theory resulted from a review of the literature on job attitudes from 1900–1955, performed by Herzberg and his staff. Although clear-cut principles did not emerge from the research, Herzberg noticed that the things that people said they liked about their jobs were different from the things they said they disliked. This important insight suggested the possibility that two sets of factors were in operation instead of the single set traditionally supposed. In other words, job satisfaction was an entirely different problem from job dissatisfaction. Subsequent research was designed to test out this hypothesis.

In 1968, in the *Harvard Review*, Herzberg summarized twelve investigations based on asking employees to report on events that lead to extreme dissatisfaction (unhappiness) and extreme satisfaction (happiness) on the job.[8] The results are shown in Fig. 4–5.

It is quite obvious from the two lists that the factors that cause dissatisfaction are not the same ones that produce satisfaction. The opposite of satisfaction, it appears, is *not* dissatisfaction. More accurately, the opposite of satisfaction is *no* satisfaction. Likewise, the opposite of dissatisfaction is *no* dissatisfaction. This distinction is more than mere semantics; it offers an important key to understanding the nature of man's needs.

Figure 4-5   Job Satisfiers and Dissatisfiers.

Events that lead to extreme satisfaction	*Events that lead to extreme dissatisfaction*
Achievement	Company policy and administration
Recognition (earned)	Supervision
Work itself	Relationship with supervisor
Responsibility	Working conditions
Advancement	Salary
Growth (psychological)	Relationship with peers
	Personal life
	Relationship with subordinates
	Status
	Security

Two sets of dynamics are at work when we consider human satisfaction. Each operates independently of the other. One is related to man's need to avoid pain from the environment. The other is related to the need to experience psychological growth. Both sets of needs require gratification if real happiness is to be achieved. It is possible, however, to achieve gratification of one set of needs and not the other. This is true in an individual's personal life as well as his or her work life. The following examples illustrate the two-dimensional nature of human satisfaction.

- The disenchanted school teacher: "I love teaching kids, but I can't afford to."

- The unionized assembly-line worker: "The company and my union take good care of me, but I hate the daily routine."

- The well-compensated, autonomous executive: "This is a great place to work, and each day is a rewarding adventure."

Although the teacher's need to experience growth is receiving adequate attention, the need to be free of pain from the environment is not. The reverse is true for the assembly-line worker. The environment is satisfactory, but there are few opportunities for gratifying the need for challenge, achievement, and growth. The executive is fortunate indeed to have the best of both worlds, experiencing gratification on both dimensions.

Herzberg distinguished between these two sets of needs by referring to one set as hygiene factors and the other as motivator factors. Sufficient hygiene (sometimes called maintenance factors) keeps the work environment from causing pain. Sufficient motivators help a person gratify the desire to continue growing. It should be noted (refer to Fig. 4–5) that the hygiene factors relate to items that surround the job—factors that are extrinsic to the actual work being performed. The motivator factors are all tied to the work itself—they are part of what the employee actually does.

To check your understanding of the Motivator–Hygiene distinction, go through the following list and identify each item as either a motivator factor or a hygiene factor.[9] Some items have elements of each, depending on how they are used. You can check your responses by referring to the Notes at the end of the chapter.

_____   A storewide golf/tennis outing

_____   An opportunity to participate in opening a new division

_____   A fifth week of vacation to recognize length of service

_____   A numbered parking space close to the store entrance

_____   Being included in an important planning meeting

_____   A well-written, well-communicated set of personnel policies and procedures, including an employee handbook

_____   A coat of paint for a person's office

_____   A difficult problem to solve, requiring long hours of work and distant travel

———   A wage program to ensure that equitable pay is given for all jobs within the company, and that wages are competitive for similar work in other companies

———   A goal-oriented, participative performance appraisal interview

Insufficient hygiene causes employees to be dissatisfied. Inadequate benefits, poor working conditions, an inconsiderate boss—all generate complaints, frustration, turnover. When these factors, or other hygiene matters, are corrected—the benefits are made competitive, the working conditions are brought up to some standard, the boss becomes more understanding—the sources of dissatisfaction begin to dissipate. But are employees more motivated? Do they work harder as a result? No! If they do, the effect is of short duration. Providing for an individual's hygiene needs will not make him or her more dedicated, more productive, more job satisfied. That is accomplished only by increasing the motivators in the job—the challenge, earned recognition, growth opportunities.

Traditionally managers have expected hygiene factors to produce motivated behavior. When attention to these factors fails to work, managers either are disappointed or feel that they need to provide more hygiene. Eventually, when the organization can no longer afford the situation, managers blame their failure on the "new breed" or give up entirely and work at finding ways to reduce or eliminate the human element in the task to be accomplished.

If managers want more motivated behavior to occur, they must be prepared to address themselves to those elements of the job that can produce job satisfaction. This means a closer look at the work they are asking people to perform. It should also be noted that the list of motivators in Fig. 4–5 is in descending order of occurrence. In other words, employees report having many more opportunities for achievement than opportunities to experience growth. Yet the motivators that bring forth the greatest commitment of energy from people are those at the bottom of the list. This means that although all of the motivators are useful, responsibility, advancement, and growth deserve closer scrutiny and positive exploitation.

CAN HYGIENE BE IGNORED?

The discussion of Self-Actualization and Motivators may lead a manager to assume that lower-level needs (hygiene) are not important. If the desire to achieve is such a powerful energizer, can we then forget pay, benefits, and working conditions? The answer is unequivocally no. Hygiene factors must be considered; they must be kept in adequate supply. When hygiene is allowed to deteriorate, enormous amounts of employee energy can go into griping and foot-dragging. If the organization is nonunion, the danger of becoming unionized increases substantially.

As Herzberg has so aptly put it, employees perpetually ask themselves two questions about their jobs: "Am I being well treated?" (hygiene) and "Am I being well used?" (motivation). Managers must be prepared with answers to these questions.

BRINGING MASLOW AND HERZBERG TOGETHER

Most managers, after hearing about Maslow's Hierarchy and Herzberg's M–H Theory, are quick to draw a relationship between the two.[10] That relationship is depicted in Fig. 4–6. This insight is impor-

Fig. 4-6   The Relationship of Herzberg to Maslow.

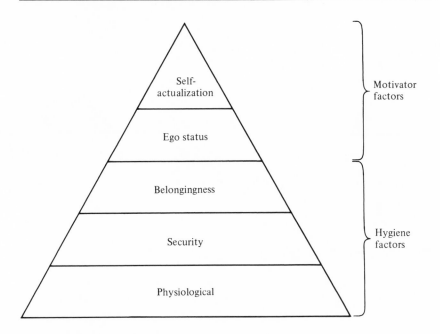

tant because it underscores the manager's responsibility for arranging the work environment to help employees move as quickly as possible through the lower needs levels so they are prepared to focus their efforts on the motivators available in the job. Again, a win–win situation is created for both the individual and the organization.

JOB ENRICHMENT

The real payoff of the M–H Theory is its application to the process of job enrichment. If employees will respond more energetically and enthusiastically to motivational opportunities in their jobs, then it follows that one of the manager's responsibilities is to put the appropriate quantity and quality of motivators into the work the people are asked to do.

If we consider the historical approach to work, we will see that many of the elements that could produce highly motivated behavior have been systematically removed. Figure 4–7 suggests that much of the more motivating aspects of jobs have been given to supervisors or staff departments. Although this has been done for the sake of efficiency, expertise, and cost-effectiveness, the unfortunate by-product has been the creation of mind-deadening, motivation-deficient work. Job enrichment, simply put, is the reversal of this historic process.

Figure 4-7   Historical View of Changes in Work.

Non-exempt Jobs Prior to 1850*	Non-exempt Jobs After 1850
Planning	_____
Organizing	_____
Implementing	Implementing
Controlling and Evaluating	_____

* Beginning of the Industrial Age

What Managers Want from Their Employees

If we consider first what we would like to have result from the enrichment process, the later steps seem logical. All managers are concerned about the following outcomes and will spend varying amounts of time trying to achieve them.

- Increased quantity of employee output
- Improved quality of the product or the service
- Greater satisfaction with the organization
- Reduced tardiness, absenteeism, and voluntary terminations
- Increased interest, cooperation, and loyalty
- Increased self-management (to reduce the need for supervision)

Our hope then is that at least some of these objectives, if not all of them, might be obtained by expending the time, effort, and money required to redesign a job. It should be noted that these are all needs the *organization* has. They may or may not coincide with particular needs employees bring with them to work.

What Employees Want from Their Jobs

The next question that might be asked, then, is what do people want from their work that they may not be getting in sufficient quantity? Many studies have been done in this area, but it is safe to generalize that three ingredients must always be present if employees are to respond positively to the organization's objectives.

1. The work must be perceived by the employees as being meaningful.
2. The employees must clearly recognize the results they are accountable for.
3. The employees must receive appropriate and timely feedback on those results, good or bad.

Seems simple enough. The difficulty is in designing and maintaining these characteristics of enriched jobs when we are constantly under seige by the contemporary forces of uniformity, unanimity, and efficiency.

Two-Stage Job Enrichment

In Stage 1, the first question for the manager to consider is, Which job or jobs could benefit from the enrichment process? Many more jobs than we might ordinarily consider have the potential to provide their holders with greater satisfaction and the organization with increased productivity. Those jobs locked into an automated, high-technology environment may be difficult, and in some cases impossible, to alter. Yet *all* jobs can probably benefit to some extent from an enrichment effort. Managers should consider all of the jobs reporting to them as having the *potential* for enrichment, until proven otherwise.

The next focus, which involves more time and effort, must be given to the analysis of how the job(s) is presently being done. This would include a formal (or informal) but systematic exploration, with the employee(s), covering the procedures, tools, reports, scope of authority, timetable, interpersonal relationships, and anything else that impinges on the work being done. The time given to analysis should be open-ended; that is, enough time should be allotted to the activity so that the employee and the manager feel confident that most of the important elements of the job have been discussed. Some note-taking during the discussion would be helpful later.

Job enrichment consultants or personnel department executives could be procured to go through the analysis portion of the process. The result would probably be a proliferation of forms and procedural requirements. In the opinion of these authors, the process is often better left in the hands of the manager and the employees, even though the result might seem less professional.

Stage 2 of the enrichment process involves looking at the data collected in the first stage and applying six simple principles of job enrichment. This can be done by the manager alone or in concert with the employee, the latter being our recommendation. Without the employee's input, the manager is apt to increase the employee's resistance to making needed changes when the enrichment process is completed. Allowing the employee's input will help ensure feelings of ownership and cooperation.

Six Important Principles of Job Enrichment

Principle One: Provide whole, natural units of work.   Much of the work done today has lost its meaning because it is only a small piece of the larger, complex final product. Employees find themselves doing fragments, middles of a job, seldom seeing the beginning or end of their efforts. It is hard to feel a sense of pride in your work when you are *The Blue Copy Gal* or the *Ticketer, Line A.*[11] To the extent possible, put the pieces back together again so an employee can feel responsible for a whole, natural unit of work. The process could involve the elimination of unnecessary tasks, or the combining of others, or the adding back of planning and evaluating activities, or some combination of all of these.

Principle Two: Provide Individual Accountability (What I do matters).   When people work on the individual pieces of many jobs, it is difficult to feel accountable for the outcomes of the work. A relinking of individual effort with the final product is in order. A customer service clerk prepares and signs a response to the customer, instead of sending a form letter. He or she then follows through on it until the matter is resolved. The salesperson or the packer puts a card with his or her name on it into the package. The waitress signs her name to the check. The connection between what I do and what I produce is established.

Principle Three: Build in participation in the planning process (My opinions count).   People feel a sense of ownership in what they have helped to create. The manager must be sensitive to opportunities for employee participation at each stage of the work flow.

Principle Four: Build in challenge (My work taxes my mental and physical capacities).   Much of work design has been aimed at eliminating the harder parts of the job. This has been done to simplify training new workers and to make it easier to fill in for absent employees. Considering the levels of education and sophistication brought by increasing numbers of employees to their jobs today, making work easier runs counter to what they are looking for. Most people today are in search of stimulating, challenging tasks to perform. They seek tougher, more thought-provoking assignments, not simpler, mind-numbing time-killers.

Principle Five: Provide greater autonomy (I'm trusted to work on my own).   Supervision should be withdrawn as quickly as the employee demonstrates the necessary psychological and job maturity. Moving toward fuller independence should be a guiding principle, much as effective parents should allow their children to grow and eventually be on their own.

Principle Six: Open up channels of feedback (Tell me how I'm doing. I can take it!).   Knowledge of results, good and bad, is an effective reinforcer. Most organizations operate under an avalanche of data. Recognizing the competitive requirements of the company, make available as much of this feedback as possible to employees.

Job Enrichment, A Continuing Activity

Because job requirements and individual needs and capacities are in a continuing state of flux, it is safe to say that job enrichment is always in a state of becoming. Managers who are concerned with sustaining a high level of motivation in their work groups will need to be always on the alert for enrichment opportunities.

MONEY AS A MOTIVATOR

The discussion about the motivational value of money continues unabated.[12] Many managers overestimate the importance of pay to their subordinates. When managers rank the job factors in Fig. 4–1, pay is almost always ranked number one. And yet there is no evidence to indicate that *just* raising pay levels leads to higher productivity.[13] According to Lawler's review of the literature, pay is rated about third by employees.[14] Herzberg's findings show pay ranking sixth. The American Research Corporation reports that income level appears to have little effect on job satisfaction. Eighty-nine percent of those surveyed who were earning *more* than $15,000 annually expressed satisfaction with their jobs. Eighty-two percent earning *less* than $15,000 said they were satisfied. Statistically, there was no significant difference.[15]

Why, then, do so many managers consistently view pay as the number one item that will produce more motivated behavior? Possibly because pay is among the items most frequently discussed by employees. Perhaps because managers sometimes project their own personal pay concerns into subordinate pay issues.

But money is a complex stimulus. People have varying reactions to it depending on their need level (in the Hierarchy), on their current pay level, the type of organization they are working in, the style of living they want to achieve or maintain, and many other factors. In short, the importance of pay to an individual is *not* fixed.

Viewed from the Maslow model, it is possible to imagine pay being instrumental in satisfying needs at every level on the Hierarchy. It is more likely to satisfy strongly felt physiological, security, and esteem needs than social or self-actualization needs.

Looked at from Herzberg's M–H Theory, money provides short-term gratifications. Furthermore, he says, it is like heroin—it takes more and more to achieve less and less effect. At some point, the system may not be able to provide money in sufficient quantity to make any real difference in an employee's willingness to expend energy to achieve organizational goals.

Real thrust and *sustained* drive on behalf of the organization seems to come from other factors. Consider, for example, the last time you, as a manager, received a pay increase. Assuming it was in line with what you thought you deserved, how long did the "motivational effect" last? One week? Two months? There was no effect? Doubtless there is some effect on all of us, but as we quickly escalate our standard of living we start looking toward the next increase to help support it. Imagine the satisfaction hourly paid employees receive from their increases.

Money, to be an effective motivator, must be administered in large doses, much larger than most organizational financial systems are prepared to distribute. Even if money were the best motivator, managers generally have so little control over how much will be given or when it will be given that it would be foolish to rely on it exclusively.

The usefulness of money as a motivator can be dramatically im-

proved through various administrative strategies; e.g., tying it directly to the accomplishment of specific, measurable, performance
objectives. In addition, these objectives must be perceived as being
within the employee's scope of influence.

Does this mean we are recommending that managers downplay
the importance of pay? Absolutely not. To provide maximum motivational value, however, pay programs must meet three criteria.
These have been well validated by research.

1. Pay must be perceived by employees as internally and externally
   equitable.

2. Pay programs, including increases, must be administered fairly
   and in a timely manner.

3. Pay increases must be *visibly* tied to performance, with the best
   performers receiving proportionately more than the weaker
   performers.

RELATIONSHIP OF MOTIVATION STYLE TO MANAGEMENT STYLE

Like communication style, motivation style may be considered a
component or an element of management behavior in general. Because this is the case, managers can expect to find a relationship
between their overall management style and the ways in which they
attempt to influence the motivational climate for their subordinates.
For example, an assistant store manager, working for a strong, task-
oriented boss (9,1) might well consider leaving the company. His
boss allows him no room to think or plan on his own, although he has
strong needs to express himself and to experience some degree of
self-actualization. The boss, because of her own style, assumes that
people want clear, firm direction, that they work to earn a paycheck
and are anxious to keep their jobs. She doesn't recognize the higher-
level needs her assistant is experiencing. (In chapter 7 we will show
how the various motivational styles and relative emphasis on Hygiene
vs. Motivator factors relate to each of the management patterns.)

KEEPING MOTIVATION IN PERSPECTIVE

Virtually everything a manager and the organization do (or don't do) will affect an employee's short- and long-term expenditures of energy on behalf of organizational goals. The left-hand side of Fig. 4–8 presents a variety of factors affecting individual motivational levels. The list could be longer. *Motivation* is a term with many facets. No manager could be expected to be expert in handling all of these factors optimally for each employee during his or her organizational life.

Often we assume that finding one motivational key or two will go a long way toward solving our productivity problems with those who work for us. The right-hand side of Fig. 4–8 suggests the key factors affecting an employee's output. Motivation is but one of the twenty-one listed, and there are others. Both motivation and productivity are complex issues for which there are no quick and easy answers. But that, of course, is what makes the managerial job so fascinating.

Figure 4-8   Forty-two factors affecting motivation and productivity.[16]

Factors Affecting Human Motivation (21)	*Factors Affecting Productivity (21)*
Nature, frequency, and timing of reinforcement	Organization's technological sophistication
Recognition for substantial accomplishment	Individual job performance
Opportunity to choose	Individual ability, education, training, experience
Support and assistance from manager	Individual job knowledge, skill levels
Level of participation in planning and goal-setting activities	Individual motivation
Understanding how individual effort affects the whole	Physical working conditions
Clear managerial expectations	Individual values, perceptions, and needs

Figure 4-8   Forty-two factors affecting motivation and productivity.[16] *(Continued)*

Factors Affecting Human Motivation (21)	*Factors Affecting Productivity (21)*
Clear and appropriate responsibilities	Personal aspiration level
Appropriate, extrinsic rewards	Economic climate/personal situation
Clear opportunity to satisfy most important personal needs	Social relationships on the job
Recognition of unique strengths and weaknesses through individualized supervision	Organization structure
Immediate and appropriate feedback on results	Overall leadership climate
Confidence expressed by supervisor	Boss's management style
Employee's ability to accomplish task	Organization efficiency
Achievable, measurable objectives and goals	Personnel policies
Climate of trust/openness	Organizational/managerial communication
Relevance and meaning of work	Size of organization
Concerned and energetic supervision	Cohesiveness of work group
Challenging work assignments	Clarity of work goals
Opportunities for growth, advancement	Relationship with boss
Appropriate levels of performance pressure	Union

NOTES
(Chapter 4)

1. Frederick Herzberg. "One More Time: How Do You Motivate Employees?" *Harvard Business Review* **46** (1968): no. 1, p. 56.

2. *Gallup Opinion Index,* Report #94, April, 1973. Although the Gallup data was collected in 1973, there is no reason to believe the situation has improved. William D. Heier of Arizona State University interviewed 692 working men and women and found that 57% admitted that they did not do a fair day's work. See "Commitment Must Replace Loyalty, Says Researcher," *Training,* October, 1980, **17,** no. 10, p. 23.

3. Charles N. Weaver. "What Workers Want From Their Jobs," *Personnel,* **53,** no. 3, May-June, 1976, AMACOM, N.Y., N.Y.

4. A. H. Maslow. "A Theory of Human Motivation," *Psychological Review* **50** (1943): pp. 370–396.

5. This case is from the *Supervising by Design* Seminar, Organization Design & Development, Inc., Gladwyne, Pennsylvania.

6. A. H. Maslow. *Toward a Psychology of Being* (D. Van Nostrand, New York, 1968), p. 153.

7. *Ibid.,* p. 26.

8. Herzberg. "One More Time: How Do You Motivate Employees?" pp. 57–58.

9. This is part of an exercise from the *Managing by Design* Seminar, Organization Design & Development, Inc., Gladwyne, Pennsylvania.

10. Herzberg himself denies this relationship. See Frederick Herzberg, *The Managerial Choice* (Dow Jones-Irwin: Homewood, Illinois, 1976), pp. 316–317.

11. "Blue Copy Gal" is the job title given to an accounts payable clerk whose sole responsibility consists of filing and maintaining the blue colored copy of payment orders. "Ticketer, Line A" refers to a person (historically female) whose sole responsibility is to place price tickets on shoes for shipment to stores. An automated line brings the unticketed shoes to her. Women on lines B, C, D, etc., perform identical work.

12. Berkley Rice. "A Simple Solution to Job Motivation: More Money," *Psychology Today* **13** (1980): no. 12, pp. 16–17.

13. Edward E. Lawler III. *Pay and Organizational Effectiveness,* (McGraw-Hill: New York, 1971), p. 67.

14. *Ibid.,* p. 42.

15. *American Families 1980,* American Research Corporation, Newport Beach, California, 1980, p. 26.

16. Motivation factors adapted from Dean R. Spitzer, "30 Ways to Motivate Employees to Perform Better," *Training Magazine* (March 1980), pp. 51–56. Productivity factors adapted from Robert Sutermeister, *People and Productivity* (McGraw-Hill: New York, 1969).

Performance Management

. . . in the long run, the executive who makes the greatest contribution to his corporation is the one who is able to release and develop the potential of the human resources that are his company's principal asset.

MALCOLM KNOWLES[1]

There are many ways to define the manager's organizational role. Perhaps one of the most useful is to view the manager as the facilitator of other people's job performance. Through various strategies, the manager enables those who work for him or her to accomplish their current job requirements, as well as to prepare for future assignments.

Figure 5-1 illustrates the Performance Management cycle. It should be observed that performance management is an ongoing process, not a single event or series of events. The activities of the

Fig. 5-1   The Performance Management Cycle.

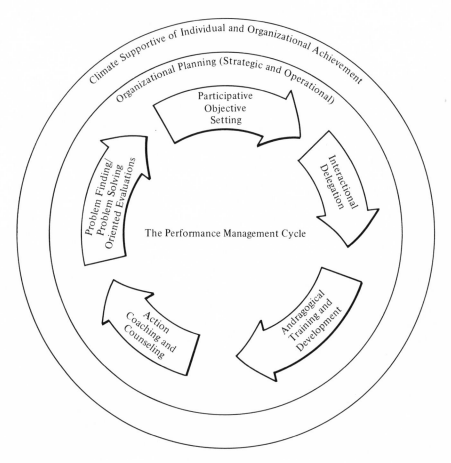

process are pictured as five continuous, flowing, overlapping, and interacting phases. The five phases are Participative Objective Setting; Interactional Delegation; Andragogical Training and Development; Action Coaching and Counseling; and Problem Finding/Problem-Solving Oriented Performance Evaluation. The operation of the five phases is related to both short- and long-range organizational plans and goals. The entire process functions most effectively when the organizational climate is supportive of individual achievement and provides the appropriate rewards.

Although the five phases—objective setting, delegation, training and development, coaching and counseling, and evaluation—are not new to the art and science of management, an executive who manages by design will approach them somewhat differently.

PARTICIPATIVE OBJECTIVE-SETTING

Effective performance management begins with the clear and full definition of the results a manager expects employees to achieve. Ideally, these results will be the logical extension of both strategic (future-oriented) and operational (day-to-day) organizational planning. The establishment of individual work objectives may be thought of as the translation of general organizational planning and goal-setting to the level of individual work activities. Unless this occurs with regularity, clarity, and in depth, there can be little assurance that the broader organizational goals will ever be reached.

How each manager makes this translation has important ramifications for both the individual employee and the organization as a whole. A Theory-Y-oriented manager, for example, will see the objective-setting process as a joint venture. Participation of both parties will characterize the process, because the manager considers the employee to be a valuable resource and knows that people find greater satisfaction in having their opinions taken into account as opposed to being directed with no questions asked. An open, confronting climate will prevail when the manager shares ideas and at the same time actively solicits input from the employee. Both individuals will adopt a problem-solving attitude, looking for creative solutions from every available source.

By contrast, Theory-X-oriented managers will think of objective setting as *their* domain. (*Managers* plan, organize, and evaluate work—not subordinates.) The climate established by these managers is likely to be directive and closed. They will seek little input from their employees because they believe that workers are not looking for involvement. They are motivated to produce when they get clear, consistent instructions from their managers, spelling out, in detail, what is to be accomplished.

Managers can choose from a variety of objective-setting systems. One of the more useful and popular approaches has been Management by Objectives (MBO).[2] MBO may be defined as an integrated management system that provides a structured and disciplined method to aid an organization in accomplishing its goals. The primary purpose of MBO is to clarify *what* is to be achieved, communicate this to the employees responsible, and provide a concrete method for evaluating the actual work accomplished in comparison to the initial plans set.

The following five statements are examples of objectives retail merchandise managers might have.

1. The sales volume of Junior Coats will be increased from $400,000 to $450,000 for the fall season.

2. The gross margin for the entire division for next year will be improved from 41.3% to 42.0%.

3. Markup for the spring season will be maintained at 48.5%.

4. The assistant buyer in Housewares will be qualified, as judged by his DMM and GMM, to be placed on the buyer candidate list for the fall.

5. The annual shortage for the Domestics department will be reduced to 2.5% by the end of the next calendar year.

All five objectives above have these characteristics:

- The statement is highly specific about *what* is to be accomplished.

- The statement is *results*- or output-oriented.

- The results described are *measurable* so that anyone can observe whether the objective has been achieved.

- The action is *time-bounded*, that is, what is to be achieved will be completed by a certain date.

Although these examples are out of the context of the actual work environment, a sound objective would be one that was both realistic and attainable, yet had sufficient "stretch" built into it so that employees would have to push themselves beyond "average" performance to reach the objective.

However well constructed objectives may be, the key ingredient that makes MBO work is employee involvement. Unless objectives are jointly established and renegotiated when necessary, the employee will feel little commitment or responsibility to achieve them. If the boss establishes the objectives for the employee, then they are the boss's objectives. If the employee participates, the probability is significantly increased that the objectives will be taken personally and seriously.

Many organizations have experimented with MBO. In those where only lip service to the MBO program exists, the entire process is seen as an annual chore, an interruption to the manager's real work. In these situations, the objective-setting is being done at the top and passed down the line for execution. Following their establishment, little attention is paid to their existence until performance review time. Suddenly the objectives reappear and are used to judge the employees positively or negatively. The real benefit of the MBO system is lost to the manager, the employees, and the organization.

In other organizations where MBO has become a viable management system, participation and negotiation are the hallmarks of the process. The objectives become a focal point for discussion, creative thought, and measurement of progress. In other words, the objectives become part and parcel of the management and organizational climate.

INTERACTIONAL DELEGATION

Once work objectives have been mutually agreed upon, the manager must delegate sufficient responsibility and authority for carrying out the activities necessary to achieve the objectives. The second phase of the performance management cycle, therefore, becomes the delegation phase.

Of all of their organizational activities, managers most often report feeling a sense of inadequacy when it comes to handling the delegation process. Managers have heard that they should "delegate more." They have often tried, with disappointing results. Perhaps the single greatest cause of delegational failure is the "all-or-nothing" approach managers use. Responsibility for a project is delegated and then weeks or months later, the project is incomplete or substandard. Meanwhile, the manager has checked casually with the employee from time to time. The employee, not wishing to appear incompetent, reports that everything is O.K.

Delegation is a gradual process that must be thoughtfully synchronized with the employee's readiness to assume responsibility for specific task accomplishment. Norman Maier has suggested a four-stage model.[3] Figure 5–2 suggests a relationship between the four stages of delegation, the employee's specific maturity level[4] to accomplish a given task objective, and the involvement of the manager. An employee at the lowest level of maturity, for example, would be a candidate for the first stage of delegation. The manager would delegate a specific duty or duties only. Involvement with the employee would be substantial during this stage. As the employee grows in

Fig. 5–2   The Delegation/Supervision Process.

Stage 1	Stage 2	Stage 3	Stage 4
Delegate specific duty(ies) only	Delegate duties and anticipate the Manager's thinking; check first before taking specific action	Delegate duty(ies) and participate in planning, problem-solving, and evaluation	Full delegation
M1	M2	M3	M4

More supervision   Less supervision maturity, delegation of stages 2 and 3 would be appropriate, with stage 4 signaling complete responsibility for a project. Correspondingly, the manager's involvement would decrease as stage 4 became appropriate.

Figure 5–3 illustrates Maier's delegation model applied to an assistant buyer's job. Once again, we are suggesting a careful management of the transaction. If an employee is unable to respond to a particular stage of delegation, the burden is on the manager to reassess the employee's maturity level. The analysis might suggest the need to drop back to an earlier stage of delegation, providing additional preparatory training, coaching, or counseling. Instead of an all-or-nothing event, delegation is a highly *interactional* process requiring continual assessment, behavioral adjustment, and reassessment.

Figure 5–3 Maier–Hersey–Blanchard Combined Delegation Model.

Maturity Level	*Stage*	*Example*
M1	1	Buyer asks assistant to call branches for a stock count
M2	2	Assistant suggests quantities to be distributed to branches, but checks before taking action
M3	3	Assistant participates in developing plan for the department
M4	4	Assistant plans, buys and merchandises a classification

ANDRAGOGICAL TRAINING AND DEVELOPMENT

The third component of the Performance Management Cycle is training and development. It is important to recognize that a single, distinct, and sequential component of the cycle may not always be apparent during an on-going boss–employee relationship. All of the components could be in operation at any given point in time, for various activities. The five phases of the cycle are delineated mainly for their descriptive value.

Most managers have a traditional conception of their training and development responsibilities. Employees need information and skills to perform their tasks and the manager's job is to transmit the required expertise. The employee is seen as an empty vessel into which managers pour as much know-how as time permits. This view of training and development is perpetuated by conventional training departments and institutionalized learning, to which everyone is exposed for a major portion of their lives.

The theory of an employee as an empty vessel sets up managers for an unending training involvement that is nearly impossible to fulfill, given their diverse management duties and the high rate of turnover. In addition, many jobs have become so complex, because of the information explosion, that training and development requirements often go well beyond what managers and training departments can offer, even under the best of circumstances.

Because of these and other factors, the goal of training and development is beginning to shift toward stimulating employees to engage in a career-long process of discovering, on their own, what they need to know, through a variety of means. Accordingly, what is to be learned is gradually becoming more the responsibility of the employee while the role of the manager is evolving to that of a climate setter and facilitator, rather than a trainer and educator.

The concept of andragogy may serve to clarify the change in the manager's training role. Malcolm Knowles, a key figure in the field of adult education, makes a distinction between the teaching of children (pedagogy) and the teaching of adults (andragogy). The distinction is based on the assumptions made about the learner and the conditions needed for learning to occur. Figure 5–4 summarizes these differences.[5]

Despite the shifting nature of employee needs, many managers continue to function like pedagogues, teaching their employees as though they were children. This is consistent with their own past learning experiences and with other elements of their management style. They see their employees as dependent on them for job knowledge and skill; undervalue their experiences from other life situa-

Figure 5-4 Andragogy versus Pedagogy.

Learner Characteristics	Children	Adults
Self-concept	Dependent on others	Autonomous
Life experience	Shallow or missing	Rich resource for learning
Readiness to learn	Teacher decides appropriate time and material	Learners decide what they need
When will I use what I've learned?	Learning prepares me for the future	Learning helps me to solve my current problems

tions; decide what will be learned and when that learning will take place; and attempt to fill these needs with conventional techniques such as the lecture in the four-wall classroom.

Managers who behave as andragogues, on the other hand, see employees as being primarily self-directed and independent; recognize their past experience as an important base for new learning; help the employees decide what they need to know in order to function effectively in the job; and deal with the employees' immediate job-related problems, using a variety of available means. Rather than focusing mainly on *what* is to be learned, the andragogue-manager is concerned with *how* the learner can develop a set of procedures for independently acquiring the needed information and skills.

ACTION COACHING AND COUNSELING

Coaching and counseling, the fourth phase of the Performance Management Cycle, is probably the most frequently used of the four activities. Most managers do some coaching and counseling every day.

Coaching usually focuses on informally helping the employees to improve their job knowledge and/or job skill. Counseling is typically directed at problems of attitude, behavior, motivation, or interpersonal relationships.

On the surface, coaching and counseling appear natural enough, and managers generally have few concerns about their skills in this area. On the other hand, the apparent simplicity may cause managers to shortchange the process. Experience demonstrates that a few improvements in planning a coaching or counseling session can often dramatically improve the results.

The following is a five-step plan to make the entire coaching/ counseling process more effective for both the manager and the employee.

STEP 1. Plan the session, even if only a few minutes are taken to decide on objectives and to gather some pertinent facts and figures.

STEP 2. Approach the meeting with candor and openness. Your perceptions may be modified or changed completely during the session as a result of the employee's views.

STEP 3. Follow a problem-solving line of inquiry. Past performance is not nearly as important as defining the problem and generating alternative courses of action for the future.

STEP 4. Whatever conclusions are reached, they should be mutually developed and agreed upon. Getting the employee to take ownership for the solution to a problem will only occur if he or she has been involved in its development.

STEP 5. The outcome of any coaching/counseling session should be an informal action plan. What have the employee and the manager agreed to do as a result of the meeting?

Coaching and counseling skills for most managers can become more productive if managers make some effort to *design* the process and its outcomes.[6]

PROBLEM FINDING AND PROBLEM-SOLVING ORIENTED EVALUATION

Often the most dreaded part of the Performance Management Cycle is the appraisal interview, which is the fifth phase. The following two examples from "Appraisal Time at Apex" illustrate why the performance appraisal is such an unsatisfying event in the worklife of both managers and employees.

Case A: Sylvia and Faith

Sylvia has been the Blouse Buyer for about six months. This is her first buying assignment, and she is anxious to do a good job. Her business has shown moderate improvement so far, but she is concerned that Faith, her Merchandise Clerical, is not keeping very accurate records. Sylvia believes this lowers the quality of the buying decisions she makes. Furthermore, Faith has been absent a good deal lately and seems to be losing interest in her work. Faith has been in the department for eight years. Sylvia is determined that she is going to "lay it on the line" to Faith in this interview. Accordingly, she is well prepared for the interview with facts and figures.

The actual interview went something like this:

Sylvia: Faith, I'm glad to have this opportunity to talk about your performance with you. I've been very concerned about some of the information you've been giving me. I think it's affecting my business negatively.

Faith: (puzzled) Oh. I thought things were going pretty well. . .

Sylvia: I know you *want* to do a good job, but I see some serious problems developing. I've spent quite a bit of time thinking about this, and I want to tell you as clearly as I can what's wrong, and what you need to do to correct these problems . . .

(Sylvia then went into a carefully documented, persuasively stated description of Faith's weaknesses and an equally well-documented, persuasively stated prescription for improvement. When she finished she mentally gave herself a "pat on the back" for her efforts on Faith's behalf.)

... And so, knowing that you have eight years invested in this store, and are interested in doing a good job, I'm sure you'll want to give serious consideration to the things I've said. After all, they are for your own good. Any particular reactions at this time?

Faith: (Suppressing her disappointment and resentment) No. I'll do my best to improve, Sylvia.

Sylvia: O.K. I'm sure that things will work out, if you'll just make some effort in those areas I've outlined.

Case B: Marilyn and Harold

Marilyn is considered a professional women's shoe buyer. She has been in her current position for twelve years and has built a substantial business during her tenure. Harold, her assistant, has been in his job for a little more than a year. Previously, he was a ready-to-wear assistant and has had some difficulty in making the transition. Harold seems capable, although some problems have developed recently. In Marilyn's opinion, he does not have quite the "sense of urgency" for a merchant, and she feels this review might be a good time to surface her observations. Harold has aspirations to become a buyer.

Marilyn has done a careful job in analyzing Harold's performance. Her strategy is to tell Harold exactly what she thinks, and then, knowing he will be upset and perhaps even angry, plans to allow him to take whatever time necessary to express his feelings. Once this is over, Harold will be ready to make some changes.

The actual dialogue went something like this:

Marilyn: Harold, make yourself comfortable. It's that time of the year again when we all have to go through the performance appraisal process.

Harold: Yes. It's been a pretty good season for me. I'm hoping that next year at this time, I'll be a buyer.

Marilyn: I hope so too, but meanwhile there are some problems that we need to talk about. I've given a great deal of thought to your work, and I want to give you as accurate an assessment as I can. Not everything, I regret to say, is as positive as I would like it to be. (Harold stiffens at this.)

(Marilyn proceeded, without interruption, to detail Harold's strengths and weaknesses as she had observed them. When she was finished, she deliberately paused to allow time for Harold to respond.)

Harold: (defensively) I'm disappointed in your evaluation. I've worked very hard this year, taking work home that you were not even aware of . . . etc., etc. . . .

(Marilyn actively listened to Harold's reasoning. Occasionally she summarized his feelings but in general tried not to arouse more controversy. Eventually, Harold, having vented his initial reactions, spoke more positively to Marilyn.)

Harold: I'm glad you brought up these things. You know I've really enjoyed working for you and respect the things you say. I'll do my best to work on the problems that you have identified. I want very much to be a buyer in this store.

Now, by way of contrast, consider Case C.

Case C: Philip and Ralph

Philip is the Housewares Buyer and is regarded as a solid merchant. In addition, he is a good trainer and usually has an executive trainee entrusted to him. Ralph, the currently assigned trainee, has been in Philip's department for the last nine months. Although he appears to have potential, his performance has been less than satisfactory: inadequate attention to detail, inaccurate paper work, poor grasp of the merchandise planning process, and assorted other problems.

Philip knows that it is his responsibility to see that trainees acquire the necessary merchandising skills. His approach to the appraisal session is to have the trainee do most of the talking.

The actual conversation went something like this:

Philip: Ralph, it's that time of the year again when we do formal performance appraisals. Helping you develop your merchandising skills is a very important part of my job.

Ralph: Good. I'm looking forward to this session. As you suggested, I've spent quite a bit of time thinking about my job and how I can improve it.

Philip: Great. We'll take as much time as we need. Where do you think we should begin?

Ralph: Well, in general, I think I've done a pretty good job.

Philip: (without committing himself) O.K. Let's focus on what can be improved, as you see it.

Ralph: Well, I've been a little bothered by the amount of paperwork required. I had no idea being an assistant would keep me tied to the desk.

Philip: What systems, specifically, do you find a problem?

(Ralph gives a detailed account of all of the paperwork systems he has had problems with.)

Philip: What can be done to improve the accuracy and the timeliness of your paperwork?

(Ralph lists several approaches he might take.)

Philip: What else should we give our attention to?

Ralph: Planning for a new season also throws me a bit. I'd like some guidance from you.

Philip: What particular area would you like more help with?

Ralph: I feel snowed when I look at the various stock levels in the store. How do you get to those numbers?

Philip: That's a good point. I'll show you how those figures are developed from past history and other factors before we plan the next season.

(The interview continued, focusing on Ralph's job and how the results could be improved. Philip probed for specifics and pushed Ralph for commitment to make changes. At the end, Philip summarized what Ralph had said and asked him to develop an action plan and a timetable to deal with the decisions made during the interview. Finally, Philip identified a few additional areas needing attention, from his point of view. The discussion concluded with both Philip and Ralph genuinely interested in making the required changes.)

The Apex cases A, B, and C represent three different approaches to performance-appraisal interviewing. Norman Maier has identified the three styles as the "Tell and Sell Method," the "Tell and Listen Method," and the "Problem-Solving Method."[7] Figure 5–5 summarizes the characteristics of each of these methods.

Case A, involving Sylvia and Faith, is illustrative of the Tell and Sell method of performance appraisal. Sylvia believes that preparation and persuasion will cause Faith to pay more attention to her record-keeping duties. Faith, for reasons unknown to Sylvia, has a different view of her past performance. But she quickly suppresses her reactions when she perceives Sylvia's intent. The promise to im-

Figure 5-5   Three Methods of Appraisal Interviewing.

Interview Characteristics	Tell and Sell	Tell and Listen	Problem-Solving
Objective of the Manager	Persuade employee to improve	Communicate evaluation, get employee's response, deal with feelings	Focus on job problems, stimulate growth, development, improvement in job performance
Assumptions of the Manager	People will correct their weaknesses if they know what they are	People change if their feelings are taken into account	Growth can occur without correcting employee's faults. Discussing job problems leads to performance improvement
Role of the Manager	Judge	Judge/ Counselor	Coach/Faciliator
Typical reactions from employees	Defensiveness, resistance, compliance or rebelliousness	Defensive, but reduced resistence to changes suggested by manager	Positive problem-finding, problem-solving behavior. Stronger personal commitment to change
Most appropriate use	M1–M2 employee maturity levels	M2–M3 employee maturity levels	M3–M4 employee maturity levels

prove masks her real feelings. In all probability, the next review will be equally disappointing to both Sylvia and Faith and may result in Faith's transfer or termination.

Case B, describing Marilyn and Harold, differs from Case A in that Marilyn expects a negative reaction from Harold. So that Harold will be able to follow her advice, Marilyn plans for Harold's need to defend and justify his past performance. She plays the role of an empathetic listener. The end result of this Tell and Listen approach is considerably better than that achieved by Sylvia and Faith because the working relationship is left intact. Some doubt, however, exists as to how committed Harold actually is to Marilyn's solutions. In both cases, A and B, it is impossible to know if the real problems have been surfaced and dealt with.

Case C, an interview between Philip and Ralph, illustrates a "Problem-Solving" approach to performance appraisal. Of the three cases, Ralph would appear to have the best opportunity to change, grow, and develop as a result of the meeting. From the beginning, Philip sets the stage for a candid and comprehensive review. Notice that the interview starts with the employee's assessment of his own performance, not with the manager's. Employees are often more critical of their own performance than their bosses are. Areas not covered by the employee can be picked up by the manager later in the interview.

The important difference between this appraisal interview and the other two is the focus on the present and future as opposed to the past. What can *we* do now to solve some of the job-related problems that may hinder your performance? The result is full exploration of the employee's performance capability and a high level of commitment to solving those problems, with the boss playing the role of a coach and facilitator.

Although the problem-solving method is a radical change from the traditional performance-appraisal interview, it is clearly more consistent with a Theory Y, andragogic style of management. In the long run, the results are far better for the employee, the manager, and the organization.

PERFORMANCE MANAGEMENT

Five phases of the performance management cycle have been described. Each phase illustrates the use of a traditional performance improvement vehicle in ways more consistent with the anticipated needs of employees and organizations in the eighties and nineties. The following is a summary of the vehicles we discussed:

- Management by Objectives with strong emphasis on employee participation and commitment.

- Interactional delegation relating an employee's task maturity level to an appropriate delegational stage.

- Andragogic training and development, emphasizing learner involvement with the entire training and development process.

- Action coaching and counseling, suggesting greater planning for what is usually viewed as an informal, everyday activity.

- Problem-solving appraisal interviewing, focusing joint manager/employee energy on finding and solving those issues that impede the employee's performance.

By using the five phases of the performance-management cycle in these nontraditional ways, managers can dramatically improve the results they obtain from their people.

NOTES
(Chapter 5)

1. Malcolm Knowles. "The Manager as Educator," *Journal of Continuing Education and Training* **2** (1972), no. 2.

2. For a far more complete discussion of MBO, see W.J. Reddin, *Effective Management by Objectives* (McGraw-Hill: New York, 1971).

3. Norman Maier. *The Appraisal Interview* (University Associates, La Jolla: California, 1976), pp. 179–181.

4. Maturity level is used in the sense of the Hersey–Blanchard Situational Leadership Model described in Chapter 2.

5. See John D. Ingalls. *Human Energy* (Addison-Wesley: Reading, Massachusetts, 1976), pp. 135–154.

6. V.R. Buzzotta; R.E. Lefton; and Mannie Sherberg. "Coaching and Counseling: How You Can Improve The Way It's Done," *Training and Development Journal* (November 1977).

7. Maier. *The Appraisal Interview*, pp. 1–19.

Building a Winning Team

*Little change happens in a group unless someone
makes a strong intervention.*

DAVE FRANCIS AND DON YOUNG[1]

Scene: A boardroom, ten o'clock Monday morning. The chairman, president and seven vice-presidents gather for their weekly business review and planning session.

Chairman: (after ten minutes of private conversation among the various members.) OK! Let's get started. We've got lots to do. Time is money. Too many meetings around here as it is. (To finance vp) Run us through the figures.

Finance VP: Beginning with last week's sales . . . (methodically reads aloud the updated financial statement. Elaborates excessively on details. Gets stuck on inconsequential points. Meanwhile other vice-presidents slouch, shift their positions, doodle, periodically check their watches.)

President: (a little before the finance vp completes his last sentence.) You know, I'm really concerned about our ability to make the spring plan . . . (the merchants around the table, sensing an impending attack, gird for battle by shuffling through reams of reports for the one special, magical sheet. The nonmerchants silently band together as if to ambush. A heated discussion begins and rises to a crescendo. People talk over each other, accusing one another of not understanding the "real" point. Conversation is rapid, impatient, intense. Ideas are quickly decapitated before they can be fully expressed. Two or three vice-presidents dominate the discussion, pushing their personal agendas, while the others become apathetic.)

Chairman: (as the noise begins to subside) We obviously need more information before we can make a decision. Since we're pressed for time, let's go on to the next item on the program and come back to this next week. (The meeting rambles on, covering several more subjects. Goals remain diffuse. No movement develops toward a solution to any problem. At times members seem more concerned with their personal status than

coming to grips with the real issues. The meeting
eventually ends with little being accomplished. Members grumble to each other about the length of the
meeting and get up to return to their individual baro-
nies. Meanwhile, pressing decisions will be made privately by one or two members of the Committee.)

The above scene is repeated again and again at every level in
organizations throughout the country. People have come to regard
the results of group effort like the proverbial camel—a horse designed by a committee. Unless something happens to change the way
most meetings are conducted, we are likely to continue producing
camels when we would really prefer horses.

An interesting piece of research involving sixty groups of people,
thirty trained in group problem-solving and decision-making, and
thirty untrained, demonstrated that by learning a few concepts and
skills, groups could dramatically improve their operating effectiveness. After two weeks of training, the thirty trained groups, when
given a problem to solve, outperformed the thirty untrained groups
on every criterion of group effectiveness.[2] In addition, half of the
trained groups outperformed their *best* resource.

It is worthwhile to look more closely at the makeup of the groups
in the study. Both the trained and the untrained groups included
experienced business managers, college students, and hospitalized
neuropsychiatric patients. Embarrassing at it might seem, the *trained*
neuropsychiatric patients significantly *outperformed* the experienced
but *untrained* business managers by a decision accuracy margin of
nearly twenty-five percent!

It seems clear from this and many other experiments with group
dynamics that collections of people working together to solve problems can do so quite effectively—often more effectively than individuals working by themselves. It is also apparent that there is nothing
inherently good or bad about groups, that they can accomplish pretty
much what their members and leaders want them to accomplish. In
short, meetings will be as useful or as useless as we choose to make
them.

It should be recognized, however, that people coming together to
solve problems and make decisions will not *automatically* do a better

job than individuals working in isolation. Effective and satisfying group work is *not* necessarily a natural human activity. Some concepts, skills, introspection, and practice are essential ingredients.

TEAMS IN CONTEMPORARY LIFE

When one stops to consider it, teams (or groups masquerading as teams) are found everywhere in contemporary society: sports, religion, politics, education, music, law, hospitals, community organizations, the family, business, civil service. The complexity of performing many tasks often requires many individuals with discrete knowledge and skill. This may be viewed as an outgrowth of our present level of technological sophistication where it no longer is possible for one or two individuals to supply all of the required expertise.

Perhaps the most obvious and ubiquitous example of teamwork in American life is the sports team. Numerous football, basketball, hockey, and other team events are watched or listened to each week by the average citizen. During a lifetime one may witness countless examples of highly skilled players, meshing their efforts in a coordinated action resulting in a win or a loss. We have come to demand exemplary, beautifully executed performance from these teams. When we do not get it, we all know what went wrong: a block missed, a play not carried through, a signal misread. We expect these teams to work hard at being effective. Those that do not quickly lose our respect.

Considering the national fervor for team sports, it is surprising to find the low level of carryover into organizational life. The fact that we observe superior teamwork week after week seems to make little difference when people gather around the conference table. Business teams, in particular, have much to learn from the playing field.

WHAT IS A TEAM?

A number of terms are used to designate a work configuration involving three or more people. For the purpose of this article, we will define a group, committee, task force, etc., as a collection of individuals who have come together for a specific, common purpose. Their combined efforts are supposed to produce a given product or service.

How effectively this collection of individuals work, how it feels about its accomplishments and about itself is often left largely to chance. No special effort is made to ensure that the best possible product emerges or that the individual members feel a sense of pride and achievement.

A *team,* on the other hand, is a very special designation awarded to a group of people who feel energized by their ability to work together, who are fully committed to a high level of output, and who care about how each member feels during the work process. A team with these characteristics must be carefully and deliberately constructed over a period of time. It will scrutinize its practices and work hard and patiently to eliminate those behaviors that block or inhibit the team's performance.

Effective team output is best explained through the concept of *synergy.* Synergy is the force that makes the whole greater than the sum of its individual parts. (That seems to contradict what we learned in high school geometry.)

Synergy might be more readily understood removed from group dynamics. Metals, for example, may increase their strength when combined in certain alloys.[3] The chrome, nickel, and steel alloy has made possible the development of the jet engine, capable of withstanding the super high temperatures needed to generate the required thrust of an aircraft. The total tensile strength of these three metals would not be great enough. Yet, when combined, the strength of the alloy reaches well beyond the simple total of the three materials. There is nothing in their individual make-up that would predict the behavior of the resultant alloy.

Synergy may also be developed by an effectively functioning group of people. Through effective teamwork, a group can generate solutions to problems that are far superior to those developed individually by its members. A synergistic decision should be the goal whenever a group of people work on the solution to a problem.

Several "survival" problems may be used with groups to demonstrate the possible synergistic effect of group problem-solving.[4] The publisher of one of these exercises reports that 650 of 802 teams, or 81%, achieved better scores as teams than they did as individual members. Synergy in group problem-solving may be said to be achieved when, through discussion, a team is able to fashion a better solution than its best resource could create on his or her own. Effectively functioning teams will produce a synergistic output more often than not.

Maturing from group to team, then, is a distinction achieved only through awareness, learning, and effort. An effective management team in action, like a well-coached football team, a well-rehearsed chamber orchestra, or a well-synchronized surgical team, is exciting to witness. The members bring a great deal of energy to their task, enjoy the process of problem-solving together, and take well-deserved pleasure from a superior end result.

WHAT CHARACTERIZES AN EFFECTIVELY OPERATING TEAM?

Most business managers have not given serious thought to their team's level of effectiveness. If they have reflected on it, usually it has been with the feeling that it is what it is, and to improve would require changing the team membership. Unfortunately, too few managers have had the opportunity to experience the exhilaration and satisfaction of being part of an effective team and therefore do not have a clear image of how their workgroup might perform if it were a true team. The following benchmarks are offered as reference points:[5]

1. Team members have a strong commitment to the achievement of organizational goals and objectives. Getting the job done, whatever it is, has top priority. Tasks are clearly understood and accepted by all. A sense of urgency, excitement, and purpose permeate the working atmosphere.

2. Team members communicate openly and frankly with each other. Each is skilled in giving and receiving constructive feedback.

3. Team members actively listen to each other. A climate of trust and understanding has been developed.

4. All members of the team participate in the problem-solving and decision-making process. Members use gatekeeping skills to ensure the involvement of the whole team.

5. Team members confront each other's assumptions in ways that do not close off further contributions. They are wary of reaching agreement prematurely. Conflict is regarded as a healthy and necessary part of the problem-solving process. It is resolved through negotiation and collaboration.

6. Team members are capable of using both competing and cooperating behaviors at the appropriate times.

7. A cohesive bond exists between individual team members and the team as a whole. An emotional investment has been made by each member. This strong unity is the basis for the energetic support of organizational objectives and goals.

8. Team members are skilled in recognizing and assuming the needed task (content) and maintenance (process) roles required for effective team operation.

9. When discussion is completed, team members feel responsible and committed to the successful implementation of the team's decisions and objectives.

10. Team leadership is appropriate. The appointed leader strongly desires an effectively operating team and takes the time to construct one. When the team is working, the leadership role may shift to whoever has the expertise, without the appointed leader feeling threatened. Power and authority are shared when possible. Much of the decision-making will be by consensus.

11. The team is capable of periodically evaluating its own effectiveness as a team. It recognizes the need to continually sense problems that hinder its effectiveness, to collect objective data to precisely define problems, to analyze data, and to modify methods of operation. The team has made a strong commitment to its own growth and maturity.

12. Team members recognize those situations where it is appropriate to work on tasks independently, in pairs, or as a team. When working as a team, members strive toward a synergistic result by consciously applying team-effectiveness concepts and skills. High-quality, individual contributions are expected and welcomed. Individual talent does not go unrecognized.

WHAT CAN BE EXPECTED
FROM TEAM BUILDING?

The process of assisting a group of individuals to work through the blockages that hinder the team's overall effectiveness is referred to as *team building*. Considering the amount of time and effort needed to transform such a group, managers should be aware of both the potential benefits and the problems.

Benefits

- Better problem definition, greater range of alternatives, better understanding of adverse consequences
- Greater commitment to the task, the team, and the organization
- Greater productivity
- Higher-quality decisions in many cases
- More open communication
- Individual growth opportunities increased from sharing of insight and knowledge
- Higher trust level
- Individuals have more positive feelings: being stroked, utilized, challenged, in on what's happening
- Greater strength and flexibility to deal with emerging problems in a rapidly changing environment
- Increased pleasure with work and associates
- Decreased organizational politics
- More stimulating meetings—climate energizing

Problems

- Time consuming
- May awaken "sleeping dogs"

- Manager may expose areas of personal weakness, feel dilution of authority

- Individuals may feel identity submerged in group

- Confidentiality jeopardized, plans revealed prematurely

- Gives people a vehicle for criticism of the manager and the organization

- Decision quality sometimes lower than if made by one or two experts

It would appear that the potential benefits outweigh the possible problems that may arise when a group embarks on the process of team building. Without question, problems will exist at the outset and continue to crop up periodically. With commitment and continued effort, however, many of these issues can be worked through and resolved. The end result will be a well-structured team, deserving of all the attendant benefits.

COG'S LADDER[6]

A group is like a living organism, moving in stages from immaturity to maturity. Each stage has fairly predictable characteristics. If managers understand these stages, they can then assess the current level of maturity of their teams and take the necessary steps to bring about growth to the next higher level. The process of team development can be accelerated by deliberately intervening in the life of a team in ways that stimulate movement toward greater maturity.[7]

Cog's Ladder is a useful model of group development, consisting of five distinct stages. In the first stage, the Polite stage, the members spend their time getting acquainted, pastiming, stereotyping other members, forming cliques. Individuals are attempting to deal with their personal comfort levels during this period.

In stage two, "Why We're Here," group members search for goals and objectives. They try to give themselves a purpose, a reason for being. In stage three, the "Bid for Power," a struggle for leadership and dominance occurs. Members compete with each other; cliques attempt to use their influence; conflict is high. During the "Constructive" stage, group members give up their attempts to control and become more cooperative. Cliques begin to dissolve. Members are willing to listen, help, and compromise. The group is most productive in the final "Esprit" stage, developing a high level of morale and team loyalty.

All groups must progress through these stages if they are to reach a more effective level of team maturity. Groups can move forward only if their members are willing to have them move forward. Growing through each stage requires that each member give up something in order to move to the next higher level of effectiveness. Recognizing that teams naturally move through levels of maturity before becoming fully effective helps the leader and the team members grasp the need to manage by design the process of growth and development.

CONTENT VERSUS PROCESS

When groups assemble to set goals, work on problems, make decisions, out of habit their focus is on the task at hand. What has to be discussed? What plans must be developed? What do we have to do to get this meeting over with? Rarely does the group give serious consideration to the feelings and reactions of its members. The most important aspect of the discussion is the *content* or the task to be accomplished. The *process* by which the task is approached receives little, if any, attention. People's anger, pleasure, commitment, frustration, sense of pride, although present, are not deliberately dealt with.

Not only are process issues present when people work in groups, they can have a discernible effect on the ultimate quality of the content and group-member willingness to support and carry out the decisions.

Team development, then, begins with the group's recognition that it will be dealing with significant process issues during its efforts to improve its effectiveness. This does not imply that content issues are unimportant. It just elevates process issues to the same level as content issues.

OPENNESS AND TRUST AS TEAM NORMS

One of the earliest process issues a developing team needs to face is the level of honesty and openness among its members. Until the team realizes that the sharing of information fully and frankly is crucial to the quantity and quality of work produced, little progress toward maturity will be made. A number of techniques are available for raising team members' awareness of the need for openness. Usually one or more exercises requiring the disclosure of information and the giving and receiving of constructive feedback can assist this process.[8]

The difficulty here stems from the fact that many people already perceive themselves as open and sharing team members. Often there is great surprise, even mild shock, when people receive their first serious feedback from others, challenging their long-held self-perceptions. Unfortunately, this self-deception is widely practiced—consciously or unconsciously—by managers who tend to see themselves more favorably than they are seen by their subordinates, peers, and bosses. Norms supporting candor and mutuality must be established and reinforced early in the game.

Closely associated with the level of openness is the level of trust among team members. Openness and trust are reciprocal conditions. When one is low, the other is likely to be low. And the reverse is true.

High trust levels are important to the team because of the effect on problem-solving and decision-making. By raising the trust level among team members, the exchange of relevant information is facilitated, objectives and problems are clarified, and the array of alternatives generated may be more imaginative. In addition to the content benefits, the team members will also experience process benefits; that is, they will be more satisfied with the team's output, have greater motivation to implement its decisions and programs, feel a greater sense of individual accomplishment and worth, and become closer as a group. There is a variety of techniques for assisting a team to increase its level of trust.[9]

CAPITALIZING ON TEAM MEMBER DIFFERENCES

There is an old organization adage that says that managers tend to hire others in their own image, thereby perpetuating the status quo. This seems to be borne out by the relative homogeneity of most management teams. Points of view and styles of behavior are remarkably similar. Individuals in the group with different orientations are usually not encouraged or appreciated. In order to survive, the deviants learn to conceal their differences and give the appearance of fitting the standard mold.

Often, however, divergent points of view can stimulate new approaches to old problems. Teams that rubber-stamp each other's thinking may reach agreement prematurely and rush headlong into a disastrous course of action. When everyone on the team holds a similar point of view, blindspots to other alternatives are likely to develop. Differences of opinion, experience, and style can produce a more balanced approach to team action. Hence, team member differences can become a valuable resource the team can deliberately cultivate to improve its output. There are methods available for providing this insight and appreciation.[10]

TOTAL PARTICIPATION

A fundamental ingredient of team effectiveness is full and willing participation by each member of the team in whatever task the group faces. Full participation improves not only the team's decision-making and problem-solving quality, it directly affects a wide range of feelings held by the members. These feelings are quickly translated into responsibility/no responsibility, commitment/no commitment, implementation rate and conviction, personal satisfaction/dissatisfaction with the organization, employee turnover, and a host of other factors. Level of participation is perhaps the single most important factor affecting team output. *Less than full participation suggests less than full utilization of the human resources available for task accomplishment.*

The effect of team member involvement or lack of it can easily be seen in a simple experiment. Give any team a problem to work on. Privately instruct one member of that team to remain silent during the discussion unless he is *directly* asked for his input by another team member. (In most groups a silent member is allowed to just remain silent.) Following the team discussion, ask the entire team, including the silent member, to individually rate such variables as feeling of responsibility, commitment, involvement, frustration, and decision quality. Those who have participated in the problem-solving will usually rate responsibility, commitment, involvement and decision quality high. Most will give a low rating to level of frustration. Silent members, on the other hand, will rate responsibility, commitment, and involvement low. Frustration level will be rated very high. Interestingly enough, decision quality is usually rated high. In other words, those who were not involved in the decision-making are saying, "Not a bad plan, but it's your plan and I'm not committed to helping you carry it out." It is axiomatic then. If you want commitment, the broadest participation feasible is required.

Having said this, how does the team ensure a high level of participation in team activity? Simply announcing that the team believes in participation will not make it happen. The answer lies in the *gatekeeping role,* which must be played routinely by each member of the team. Gatekeeping means that I am sensitive to the participation intensity of each of the team members. If their participation level is low or nonexistent, then I "open the gate" and solicit their participation. "Jack, we haven't heard from you. What's your opinion on this problem?" Sensitivity to the team's need for gatekeeping will ensure a high level of participation and all of the resulting benefits.

TEAM MEMBER ROLES

Without thinking, most group members play habitual roles. That is, they behave in ways most comfortable for them based on their past experience in group activity. This is done without regard for the needs the team might have for specific behaviors at any given time.

Just as a team has to concern itself with both content and process issues, it must also provide two kinds of behavior: *task behavior* (content) and *maintenance behavior* (process). To be an effective member of a team, members must be able to recognize the various task and maintenance roles required by the team and be able to "play" these roles when it becomes necessary.

Following are some of the important roles teams need:

Task Roles

Initiating activity

Seeking information and opinions

Giving information and opinions

Elaborating on the suggestions of others

Coordinating a number of different ideas

Summarizing what has been said

Evaluating accomplishments of the group

Recording notes on discussion

Maintenance Roles

Encouraging others

Gatekeeping

Setting standards for group
functioning

Following—going along with
others

Compromising

Expressing group feeling

Harmonizing—relieving tension

Some roles are *dysfunctional* to group progress:

Being excessively aggressive

Blocking/creating excessive
opposition

Self-confessing

Competing—being top dog

Special-interest pleading

Seeking personal recognition

Withdrawing

Entertaining

Team members may need special training in recognizing and fill-
ing the above task and maintenance roles. It would be very useful,
following a group exercise, to spend some time evaluating how the
team is functioning, which roles are being provided, and which are
missing.

PROBLEM-SOLVING STRATEGY

Characteristic of much group action is the undisciplined approach to
solving problems. Because most managers solve problems intuitively
when working alone, this habit is carried into group activity. No particular method or system is consciously employed. Through trial and
error, time and experience, problem-solving skill may improve, but
this will be by accident rather than by design.

A number of useful problem-solving models exist. Most include
careful and comprehensive problem identification, objective setting,
development of a range of possible alternative courses of action, de-
termining the adverse consequences if a particular alternative were
followed, and finally making a decision, following the alternative
most consistent with your objectives and with the least unfavorable
adverse consequences. The important point here is not which system

the team uses, but that it use *a* system. This is not to suggest that a rigid formula be followed, but to underscore the need to learn together one or more routine strategies to serve as a guide to team action.

DECISION-MAKING

Five distinct ways to make decisions are available to the manager:

- The boss decides (unilateral)
- A powerful minority decides
- A majority decides (51%)
- Consensus
- Everyone agrees (unanimity)

Each method has its advantages and disadvantages. From a team standpoint, unilateral, majority, and minority decision-making have the disadvantage of leaving some members out of the process. Decision quality and commitment may be expected to be lower as a result. Unanimity is ideal but may take more time than the team has available. Consensus decision-making would seem to offer the greatest advantage to effective team action. This means that everyone has the opportunity for input. The decision is hammered out by the team. Although not all members may be in *total* agreement, all points of view have been presented and discussed and each team member feels ready to accept and support the decision.

Teams that experiment with consensus find that decision quality and member satisfaction are very high. If that's the case, shouldn't all decisions be made by teams? The answer is *no*. The type of problem under consideration should suggest the decision-making style. If trust, commitment, and use of all the available resources are important, then the decision style should probably be consensus. If time is critical or one team member has the expertise, then a unilateral decision could be appropriate. In addition, other factors may influence the choice of decision style. An effective manager will know which style to use. An effective team will understand and support that choice, knowing that decisions that are best made by the team will be made by the team.

CRUCIAL ROLE OF THE MANAGER

Some managers, when they contemplate team development, find themselves privately concerned about the possible erosion of authority and control. Until this concern is removed or suspended, team development has little chance to occur.

If we assume that the manager is always the manager, regardless of the work configuration he or she chooses, that may offer some insight. A manager must view the development of the team as a method for increasing his or her own effectiveness and personal status. Team-building exercises imposed either from outside or without the manager's wholehearted endorsement are not likely to succeed.

In addition to the manager's personal decision to develop the workgroup into a more effective team, the members themselves need to see team development as a positive organizational strategy. The team must want to develop, understand what is meant by growth, and know something of the process they will be undertaking. Managers can do much to promote or hinder this, if they choose.

TEAM-BUILDING APPLICATIONS

The opportunities for the development of teams are endless. Some of the possible applications include

- New teams
- Helping established teams solve persistent problems and improve working relations
- Assisting two workgroups to resolve problems and work together more productively
- Strengthening a division's management to withstand a union-organizing campaign
- Solving specific problems such as high shortage, lagging sales, excessive personnel turnover
- Integrating new and old management team members
- Initiating major changes in policy and direction
- Establishing the identity of a new division as separate from the parent company

MOVING TOWARD TEAM MATURITY

Managers are conditioned to think of training programs as single events at a specific time. When the manager returns to the work environment, the training either makes a difference or it doesn't. Team development, however, must be seen as a process. It may begin with a consultant-guided workshop, but it must be carried on and given life by the team itself if the productivity and the quality of group life is to change significantly.

It may be helpful to think of teams on a maturity continuum, moving from a raw collection of individuals with diverse backgrounds and aims to a smoothly functioning, flexible work unit capable of effective individual performance, pair cooperation, or team action. Moving from immaturity to maturity is the goal of all team-building. Team maturity is a relative term. The changing nature of the organizational environment is continually presenting new obstacles and new challenges for the team to solve. During the process of maturing, the team will encounter, struggle with, and resolve many problems. As a result, teams are always in a state of becoming.

A MORE ENERGETIC, MORE SATISFYING WORK CLIMATE

The team model is not offered as a cure-all for organizational problems, but it does have many distinct advantages. Viewed from the interest of the corporation, the quality of planning, problem-solving, and decision-making can be dramatically improved by taking advantage of the synergy generated when people work effectively together. Creative energy can be exploited in the interest of improving bottom-line results at a level not previously believed possible.

From the individual employee's point of view, team development can open up new horizons at work. Teams can become stimulating, warm, rewarding facets of organizational life. As strong bonds develop between members, caring will become an important norm. People will begin to be appreciated for their differences and the unique contributions they are capable of making. A far more energetic and satisfying work climate will emerge.

NOTES
Chapter 6

1. Dave Francis and Don Young. *Improving Work Groups* (University Associates: La Jolla, California, 1979), p. 19.

2. J. Hall and M. S. Williams. "Group Dynamics Training and Improved Decision-Making," *Applied Behavioral Science* 6 (1970), no. 1, pp. 39–68.

3. Buckminster R. Fuller. *Synergetics* (Macmillan: New York, 1975), p. 6.

4. "The Desert Survival Situation," Human Synergistics, Detroit, Michigan, 1974.

5. These benchmarks have been in part suggested by Douglas McGregor, *The Human Side of Enterprise* (McGraw-Hill: New York, 1960), pp. 232–235.

6. George O. Charrier. "Cog's Ladder: A Model of Group Development," *The 1974 Annual Handbook for Group Facilitators* (University Associates: La Jolla, California, 1974), pp. 142–145.

7. For a fuller description of how a group grows and matures, see *Group Development,* 2d ed., edited by Leland P. Bradford (University Associates: La Jolla, California, 1978).

8. The Johari Window model of information-processing tendencies is very useful for helping people understand their communication style. See *Of Human Interaction* by Joseph Luft (Mayfield Publishing Co.: Palo Alto, California, 1969).

9. The TORI Group Self-Diagnosis Scale is an example of an instrument designed to assess the level of trust in a variety of groups. The data may be used to start the process of trust-building in a team.

10. The LIFO instrument, measuring life orientations, can help team members quickly understand how their differences in philosophy affect their behavior. The approach of the LIFO system is to encourage appreciation and application of the different orientations toward problem-solving and decision-making.

Managing by Design

*A new vision is emerging of the possibilities of man
and his destiny, and its implications are many...*

ABRAHAM MASLOW[1]

The underlying theme of this book has been the conviction that executives can dramatically improve their results, and become more effective managers, if they will begin to manage others by design instead of by trial and error, imitation or accident. *Managing by design* implies that thought, analysis, and planning are essential ingredients of the management process. Managing by design requires that the boss (1) be aware of his or her management behavior and its impact on others; (2) consider the various options available; and (3) choose the option that will maximize his or her own satisfaction and that of the subordinates, as well as meet the organization's productivity needs.

The following table (Fig. 7–1) represents, under five general behavior patterns, a simplified organization of the management models presented in the previous chapters. Each pattern reflects a manager's relative emphasis on the task assigned to another person to perform and his or her relationship with that individual. These two dimensions of behavior interact to create a well-defined management style. Below each general pattern, the elements or components of that pattern are specified.

For example, managers who place strong emphasis on the work to be completed, but pay little attention to the feelings and needs of their employees, may be classified under the Hi Task/Lo People category. Their philosophy of human-resource management drifts toward Theory X. Their overall approach does not vary, even though the circumstances might demand it, making them somewhat rigid in their responses to others. Their communication with others will probably be heavily laced with one-way, Critical Parent statements, coupled with little inclination to listen or to seek the opinions of others. The motivational style of these managers is focused on the hygiene factors in the work environment. They assume that people labor to satisfy their deficit needs for decent working conditions, pay, job security, benefits, and not much else. These items are emphasized when they attempt to motivate employees.

From the standpoint of participation, the Hi Task/Lo People managers prefer to plan, organize, and control the show on their own. Involving others in the problems of work is not their way of operating. Consequently, they do not use groups of people effectively when they come together in the work setting. They prefer one-to-one interactions whenever possible. Their approach to conflict is to use

Figure 7-1 Fifteen Dimensions of Management Behavior: How the Management Models Fit Together.

General Management Behavior Pattern	Hi Task/ Lo People	Lo Task/ Hi People	Lo Task/ Lo People	Medium Task/People	Hi Task/ Hi People
Philosophy of people in the work environment	Hard X	Soft X	X	X/Y	Y
Use of participation	Low	Solicitation	Low	Moderate	High
Grid style	9,1	1,9	1,1	5,5	9,9
Use of situational approach	Rigid	Yielding	Shifting to avoid responsibility	Seat of the pants flexibility	Adaptable short range
Johari Window	Heavy exposure	Heavy feedback-seeking	Both limited	Some of each	Dominant Arena
Predominant transactional style	Critical Parent	Nurturing Parent	Dependent Child	Shifts Insufficient use of Adult	Adult
Motivation style (need emphasis)	Basic and Security	Social	Security	Esteem	Self-Actualization
Hygiene versus Motivators (chief concern)	Hygiene	Hygiene	Hygiene	Hygiene and Motivators	Motivators

Figure 7-1 Fifteen dimensions of management behavior: how the management models fit together *(Continued)*.

General Management Behavior Pattern	Hi Task/ Lo People	Lo Task/ Hi People	Lo Task/ Lo People	Medium Task/People	Hi Task/ Hi People
Use of MBO	To pressure others for performance	Approves in broad terms, avoids specifics	If required by policy	Not committed; uses to extent others seem interested	Key management system
Training style	Pedagogy; no interest in development	Sees training as a way to meet people's social needs	Ignores training of others	Pedagogy; but supports popular company training programs	Andragogy; training appropriately applied to some performance problems
Delegation style	Infrequent delegation; prefers to do everything himself	Delegates whatever subordinates request	Abdicates	Delegates without regard to maturity level of subordinates	Delegates by stages and subordinate readiness; uses to promote growth

Figure 7-1 Fifteen dimensions of management behavior: how the management models fit together *(Continued).*

General Management Behavior Pattern	Hi Task/ Lo People	Lo Task/ Hi People	Lo Task/ Lo People	Medium Task/People	Hi Task/ Hi People
Performance-appraisal interview style	Tell and Sell	Tell and Listen	Mechanical discharge of company policy; may read review form	Tell, Listen, Sell	Highly interactive; problem-solving
Conflict management style	Power	Smoothing	Avoidance	Compromise	Collaboration
Decision-making style	Boss decides	What others want	Boss's boss decides or no decision	Majority rule	Consensus
Team effectiveness	Prefers 1 to 1	Group used to satisfy social needs	Loner	Uses group to determine majority interest	Uses group synergistically

their authority to resolve issues so that everyone can get back to work. Speed and efficiency are their hallmarks.

To use the table, simply locate your own behavioral preferences (task/people) and read down the column. If the concepts are somewhat unclear, refer to the appropriate chapter for an expanded discussion of the key points.

Managers who have had exposure to some management theories in the past, particularly those touted as panaceas, are often confused or disquieted when another theory is introduced. Unfortunately, many of our management and organization-development experiences leave a piecemeal impression with participants. Figure 7–1, however, suggests a solid relationship among the most popular behavioral-science models.

It should be further noted that the table is intended to be neither all-inclusive nor personally limiting. Other theories may be considered within this framework. No chart, however, will be complete enough to capture the full, rich essence of human behavior. And for that reason, the chart is suggestive rather than exhaustive.

Some people will have a strong reaction to being pigeonholed. As Maslow has observed, ". . . being rubricized is generally offensive to the person being rubricized, since it denies his individuality or pays no attention to his personhood."[2]

The purpose of a table such as this is not to rubricize managers but to provide some useful insights into their behavioral preferences and the impact these preferences might have on associates and the life of the organization as a whole. This awareness puts managers in the position of being able to choose more productive and more satisfying behaviors. They begin to understand that there are options— other ways of behaving are available. It is not necessary to remain stuck with habitual modes of dealing with task problems involving people. Changes can be made when and where that seems appropriate.

If we were to search for a model executive who *manages by design,* how would we know what to look for?[3] The behavioral sketch that follows describes a male manager. But perhaps the most important starting point would be to recognize that this model could be either male or female. Substantial research has shown that, "Women, in general, do not differ from men, in general, in the ways in which they administer the management process."[4] There are two areas, however, in which there are some differences and we will elaborate on those as we fill in our sketch.

To begin our portrait, the model manager is intensely committed to both the work to be accomplished and the needs of the people who will be doing it. Because of his unshakable belief in the willingness of people to bring their talents and energies to bear on organizational problems, he concentrates his managerial energies on involving people, at every level, in the problems and decisions that affect them. Working hard to help people utilize their potential, this manager takes the time to enlist their participation whenever it appears to be appropriate. His philosophy is heavily weighted toward Theory Y.

Although the executive who *manages by design* has a clear vision of where he wants to go with his people, he recognizes that short-term problems may require a variety of approaches. He is able to shift gears in such a way as to move each employee toward a higher level of maturity. This is not mere seat-of-the pants flexibility. It is a rational and fine-tuned method for applying specific management behaviors based on an employee's requirements. The premise here is that if the employee is not responding, then the manager is not doing an effective job of managing. Every employee has the capacity to be more productive and job-satisfied. At the same time, the manager does not lose long-range sight of the quality of the organization he wants to help create.

Understanding the importance of a free-flow of communication, this executive is extremely open and straightforward with associates, at all levels. He accepts responsibility for his own ideas and feelings and is open to the ideas and feelings of others. In fact, he willingly experiments with new ideas and encourages others to do the same. His style is characterized by a high degree of sincere interaction. Most of his transactions are Adult-to-Adult and game-free, but are crossed when there is hope of greater productivity.

There is one interesting difference in the communication style of female managers. They too are open and straightforward with their employees and their bosses, and exhibit all of the other characteristics attributed to their male counterparts. There is, however, a tendency toward less willingness to share relevant data with colleagues. While subordinates see no difference in how *they* are managed by male or female bosses, they report being somewhat less willing to solicit feedback from a female boss.

Motivation is more than just a word for this thoughtful manager. Careful analysis and planning provide a highly motivational climate for each employee. He is strongly self-actualized as an individual, and makes every effort to create opportunities for others to self-actualize in their work. Hygiene factors surrounding the job are not ignored, however. Pay, benefits, working conditions, supervisory behavior, company policy—all receive the necessary attention to minimize the sources of dissatisfaction inherent in every work situation. But the primary focus is on developing the motivators present in the job of each employee reporting to him. Job enrichment is a continuing activity.

There are no significant differences between motivational needs and style of high-achieving male and female managers. Therefore the female model also exhibits the qualities outlined above. The only apparent difference is found in females who are considered to be average-achieving managers. These women express higher needs to self-actualize and lower security needs than do male managers in the average category. More importantly, regardless of any differences that exist between the needs expressed for themselves, there is no difference in the way males and females manage the motivation of others.

And finally, the executive who manages by design is known as a team-builder. He understands the conditions under which groups of people can solve problems more effectively than individuals operating independently, or in pairs. This is not to suggest that the team method is the only approach he chooses, but when he does decide it is appropriate, his team is able to reach synergy more often than not.

Having a clear and detailed picture of what it means to be a boss who manages by design is of critical importance for each manager. Without it, changes in behavior are difficult if not impossible to make. For example, cigarette smokers who cannot imagine themselves being nonsmokers are not likely to succeed in their efforts to kick the habit. Managers who desire greater effectiveness must first *image* their new behavior, that is, see themselves operating in new and different ways with their associates before they will be able to perform effectively in the actual situation.

Changing behavior is more complex and uncertain than we might believe. Unless we realize this before we start, we are apt to be disappointed. Knowing that we have a wider range of managerial options is only the first step. The really hard part follows. Every seasoned manager has spent years acquiring the habits he or she uses to survive in the organization. It is, therefore, unrealistic to expect even strongly motivated behavior changes to occur swiftly and conclusively. Change is an uneven process. It proceeds by fits and starts, hardly ever moving smoothly or free of resistance. Managers contemplating change must be prepared for occasional backsliding.

Resistant though we might be, the complexities of the contemporary organization leave us little choice but to make some changes. For years we have promoted employees to the managerial ranks based on their task competence. Now we must insist that the same effort that is applied to acquiring task competencies also be applied to acquiring human-relations competencies.

Becoming an effective manager is a lifelong process, requiring continued theory acquisition and skill practice. The time for amateurs is long since past. The management of the working life of others is probably one of the most intellectually demanding, yet rewarding, assignments in the world of work.

No matter what its size or complexity, reduced to its most fundamental element, an organization is simply a collection of people working toward a set of shared objectives. To move any organization toward greater health requires that a majority of its executives be committed to *managing by design* as opposed to merely managing. Only this kind of effort can start the process of organizational development and growth. And nothing less than this is required to survive and prosper with the advent of *The Third Wave.*[5]

NOTES
(Chapter 7)

1. A. H. Maslow, *Toward a Psychology of Being* (D. Van Nostrand: New York, 1965), p. 127.

2. *Ibid.,* p. 189.

3. The portrait of the executive who manages by design is well supported by research. One of the most comprehensive pieces of work is reported in "To Achieve or Not: The Manager's Choice," by Jay Hall, *California Management Review* **18** (1976): no. 4.

4. Jay Hall and Susan M. Donnell, "Men and Women as Managers: A Significant Case of No Significant Difference," *Organizational Dynamics,* AMACOM, New York, NY, Spring 1980, p. 76. Other differences between male and female managers cited in the profile of a manager who *manages by design* were summarized from this article. The study included 1,916 managers, 850 females and 966 males.

5. Alvin Toffler, in *The Third Wave,* describes the current disintegration of industrial society as the beginning of the third wave. The first wave, the agricultural revolution, began about 8000 B.C. and lasted until between 1650–1750. According to Toffler, 1955 marks the recession of the industrial age, which was the second wave, and the beginning of the third wave, the new civilization. The third wave is ". . . based on diversified, renewable energy sources; on methods of production that make most factory assembly lines obsolete; on new, non-nuclear families; on a novel institution that might be called the 'electronic cottage'; and on radically changed schools and corporations of the future." (William Morrow, New York, 1980, p. 26.)

Postscript

*"The only way to gain a significant competitive edge is
through better management."*

ROBERT BLAKE AND JANE MOUTON [1]

Following a three-day *Managing by Design* seminar, many participants ask what else they might do to further their understanding of
the management process. We may suggest several courses of action,
but one we always recommend includes further exploration of the
universal models presented in the session. That can best be accomplished by a leisurely reading of the original works of some of the
most influential behavioral scientists. These are stimulating books,
comparable in many respects, to the Great Books. They are meant to
be read in their entirety.

THIRTEEN BOOKS TO INCREASE YOUR MANAGERIAL EFFECTIVENESS

Managing in the 800th Lifetime

Massey, Morris, *The People Puzzle,* Reston Publishing, Reston,
Virginia, 1979.

---

1. Robert Blake and Jane Mouton, *The New Managerial Grid* Houston, Texas:
Gulf Publishing, 1978, p. 117.

Toffler, Alvin, *The Third Wave,* William Morrow, New York, 1980.

Belief and Behavior

McGregor, Douglas, *The Human Side of Enterprise,* McGraw-Hill, New York, 1960.

Blake, Robert, and Jane Mouton, *The New Managerial Grid,* Gulf, Houston, Texas, 1978.

Hersey, Paul, and Kenneth H. Blanchard, *Management of Organizational Behavior,* Prentice-Hall, Englewood Cliffs, New Jersey, 1972.

Person-to-Person Communication

Luft, Joseph, *Of Human Interaction,* Mayfield Publishing, Palo Alto, California, 1969.

Berne, Eric, *Games People Play,* Grove Press, New York, 1954.

Morrison, James and John O'Hearne, *Practical Transactional Analysis In Management,* Addison-Wesley, Reading, Massachusetts, 1977.

Creating a Climate for Achievement

Maslow, Abraham, *Toward A Psychology of Being,* D. Van Nostrand, New York, 1963.

Herzberg, Frederick, *The Managerial Choice,* Dow Jones-Irwin, Homewood, Illinois, 1976.

Sutermeister, Robert, *People and Productivity,* McGraw-Hill, New York, 1969.

Performance Management

Lefton, Robert, *et al., Effective Motivation Through Performance Appraisal,* Wiley, New York, 1977.

Building a Winning Team

Francis, Dave, and Don Young, *Improving Work Groups,* University Associates, La Jolla, California, 1979.